M. R. De

THE
SECOND
COMING
OF JESUS

M. R. De Haan

kregel
PUBLICATIONS

Grand Rapids, MI 49501

The Second Coming of Jesus by M. R. De Haan © 1996 by
the M. R. De Haan Trust and published by Kregel Publications, P.O. Box 2607, Grand Rapids, Michigan 49501. All
rights reserved.

Cover photo: Copyright © 1996 Kregel, Inc.
Cover design: Art Jacobs

Library of Congress Cataloging-in-Publication Data

De Haan, M. R. (Martin Ralph), 1891–1964.
The second coming of Jesus / M. R. De Haan.
     p.   cm.   (M. R. De Haan classic library)
   Originally published: Grand Rapids, Mich.: Zondervan,
1944.
   1. Second advent. I. Title. II. Series: De Haan, M. R.
(Martin Ralph), 1891–1964. M. R. De Haan classic
library.
BT885.D35   1997   236'.9—dc20   96-32046
                                     CIP

ISBN 0-8254-2483-6

Printed in the United States of America
1 2 3 4 5 / 00 99 98 97

Contents

1. He Is Coming Again 7
2. That Blessed Hope 39
3. When Jesus Comes 72
4. The Mysteries of the Kingdom 93
5. The Antichrist 128
6. Peace in a World of War 150

CHAPTER ONE

He Is Coming Again

Tell us, when shall these things be? and what shall be the sign of thy coming, and of the end of the world? And Jesus answered and said unto them, Take heed that no man deceive you. For many shall come in my name, saying, I am Christ; and shall deceive many. And ye shall hear of wars and rumours of wars: see that ye be not troubled: for all these things must come to pass, but the end is not yet. For nation shall rise against nation, and kingdom against kingdom: and there shall be famines, and pestilences, and earthquakes, in divers places. All these are the beginning of sorrows. Then shall they deliver you up to be afflicted, and shall kill you: and ye shall be hated of all nations for my name's sake. And then shall many be offended, and shall betray one another, and shall hate one another. And many false prophets shall rise, and shall deceive many. And because iniquity shall abound, the love of many shall wax cold (Matt. 24:3-12).

SIGNS OF HIS COMING

The darker the day, the brighter the blessed hope of the Christian shines. The more terrible world events become and the darker the deepening gloom of civilization's coming crisis looms upon the horizon, the brighter gleams the hope of the believer in a better day, that day when —

> Jesus shall reign where'er the sun
> Doth his successive journeys run;
> His kingdom stretch from shore to shore
> Till moons shall wax and wane no more.

It is well to look back to the days of Christ's humiliation, suffering and death — there to see the awful, infinite price He had to pay for our redemption. However, the first coming of the Lord Jesus was but the first step in a series of events which will culminate in the crowning of this King Jesus with a crown of authority — not a crown of thorns. Then He will sit on the throne, not hang on the Cross.

Nothing is more certain than the personal, bodily return of the Lord Jesus to this earth. Scripture has much more to say concerning His second coming than His first. Yet millions accept the first but reject, or at least ignore, the second.

HIS COMING IS IMMINENT

We believe in the imminent personal return of the Lord Jesus Christ as the only hope of this war-torn world. The word *imminent* has been much misunderstood. When we speak of His imminent return many people think we mean the *immediate* return of the Lord. Hence they accuse those who preach it of being false prophets because Christ has not come back. By *imminent* we mean that Jesus *may* come at any time. His second coming is an undated event as far as God's revelation is concerned. We do not know *when* He is coming, but we do know that He *is* coming and *may* come at any time. The term "immediate coming" implies that He will come immediately or at some date which is determined. No well-taught Bible student attempts any such foolish speculation. There have been those in the past who have attempted it but all have failed and brought reproach upon the blessed truth of the Lord's return. Therefore, remember that while we look for Him constantly and He may come at any time, we teach this: "That day and hour knoweth no man, no, not the angels of heaven."

HIS COMING IS NEARER

We do know, however, and dare to preach that He is coming. From all the signs given in the Bible by the Lord Jesus Christ Himself, His coming is very near today. The indications predicting the return of the Lord have increased with amazing rapidity. In the twenty-fourth chapter of Matthew's Gospel there are, among others, at least nine sure signs which the Lord Jesus declares will precede His return. These nine are:

1. False messiahs and christs (vs. 5).
2. Wars and rumors of wars (vs. 6).
3. Famines and pestilences (vs. 7).
4. Earthquakes in divers places (vs. 7).
5. Anti-Semitism and Jew baiting (vss. 9-10).
6. False prophets and deceivers (vs. 11).
7. Increase of iniquity (vs. 12).
8. Apostasy and love growing cold (vs. 12).
9. The universal preaching of the Gospel (vs. 14).

Remember that the Lord gave these signs to the disciples in answer to their question: "Tell us, when shall these things be? and what shall be the sign of thy coming, and of the end of the world?" Jesus, answering, said, "Take heed that no man deceive you." Before giving His disciples the signs of His coming again, He admonished them against being deceived by men. He said there was to be an age of deception and false teaching, and then gave the nine signs of His return.

1. FALSE MESSIAHS AND CHRISTS

Never before in the history of the world has there been so much deception practiced by those who claim to be the saviours of civilization and of the world. It is said that in the last one hundred years there have been no less than thirty-six men who have claimed to be the Messiah, and these have deluded millions. Today there are an undetermined number of men and even women who claim deity, who call themselves by divine titles and say they are messiahs and christs.

2. WARS AND RUMORS OF WARS

This second sign surely needs no comment at this time. With two-thirds or more of the world in the bondage of declared or undeclared war, the world is facing the greatest military crisis in all its history. With the modern implements of war the gravity of any war is multiplied beyond computation. Amid all this carnage and war there is a constant stream of rumors of more wars. The nations which are not actually in the conflict are riven by fear and doubt. Seeing the handwriting on the wall, they, too, are preparing as feverishly for war as though they were actually at war. Today the whole world is an armed camp and sane men are shaking their heads and asking the question, "What will be the outcome of this?"

3. *FAMINES AND PESTILENCES*

These two ever follow in the wake of war. In China, millions have died of starvation and pestilence. We have received ominous reports from Europe concerning many of the peoples ruthlessly conquered by the Satan-inspired totalitarian dictators. A few months from now we may understand more fully what Jesus meant when He said, "And there shall be famines, and pestilences."

4. *EARTHQUAKES IN DIVERS PLACES*

"Earthquakes." How familiar that word sounds in the light of the recent newspaper reports from every section of the globe, many from parts of the world where earthquakes had heretofore been unknown. Scientists tell us that the number of earthquakes is rapidly on the increase. Even though it is admitted that modern scientific instruments and seismographs have made it easier to detect slight and otherwise imperceptible shocks, it is still a fact that there have been far more earthquakes in the past twenty-five years than in any other corresponding length of time in history. In view of this Jesus' words are very significant. He said, "Earthquakes, in *divers places*." The meaning of this expression is that there will be earthquakes in several places at the same time. This has never happened until recently. During the great Turkish earthquake which took tens of thousands of lives and resulted in countless millions of dollars' damage, the scientists reported that that great earthquake was not the only one which occurred on that day but with it, almost simultaneously, were shocks of varying severity felt in at least four other parts of the globe, — South Africa, Carolina, California and South America. How significant this is in the light of Jesus' words, "Earthquakes, in *divers places.*" We seem to be living in the very days of which Jesus spoke. To my knowledge — and I have searched for evidence — there is no other record in history of a similar phenomenon. Surely we must heed the words of the Saviour: "When these things begin to come to pass . . . lift up your heads; for your redemption draweth nigh."

5. *ANTI-SEMITISM AND JEW BAITING*

Jesus said, "Then shall they deliver you up to be afflicted . . . and ye shall be hated of all nations for my name's sake." As you well know, Jesus was speaking to His disciples. They were Jews and already at that time under the heel of the Roman boot, and our Lord said that in the last days they would be "hated of all nations." We realize that the ultimate fulfillment of these signs will come in the Tribulation (that period of time which will follow immediately upon the snatching away of the Church), but the premonitory signs (the beginning of these things) will precede that great event, as we shall see in a moment. Has there ever been a period in Israel's history when her condition was more precarious? Instead of one Pharaoh in the land of Egypt there are today numerous Pharaohs and Caesars in as many lands who have revived the old anti-Semitic madness. They blame all the evils and misfortunes of the world on the Jews and propagate the hellish doctrine that the salvation of the world must come as a result of the annihilation of the Jews. It is the old story with a new satanic vengeance. It is estimated that there are some 16,500,000 Jews in the world today, the bulk of them in Europe. Of these 16,500,000 there are at least 10,000,000 who are not welcome in the lands where they dwell. Undetermined num-

bers are in concentration camps, herded together in revived ghettos, while millions have been slain for no reason other than that they were Jews — of the same nation-
ality as the Lord Jesus Christ Himself. In Germany,
Italy and the conquered countries these brethren of the
Lord, according to the flesh, are driven to desperation as
the words of our Lord are being fulfilled before our very
eyes. O Christian, can you not see what God is trying to
tell us through these events? He is, as it were, shouting
that the day — that glorious day — is near at hand when
the Lord shall redeem His people Israel, plant them again
in their own land, and turn again their captivity so that
none shall make them afraid. May God hasten the glad
day!

6. *FALSE PROPHETS AND DECEIVERS*

The sixth sign given in Matthew 24 is *false prophets*.
These must not be confused with *false christs*. The two
are thus distinguished by the Lord Jesus. False christs
claim deity and lordship. False prophets are those who
come as angels of light, preaching a gospel which is not
the Gospel and presenting a plan of salvation without the
blood of Christ and without His Resurrection. They tell
men that by keeping the Golden Rule, practicing the
Sermon on the Mount, and keeping the commandments
they will be saved. Preaching and teaching a gospel of
works (fig leaves), these false prophets would have men
save themselves by their own goodness and their own
works, thus despising the sacrifice of God in the Person
of His Son on the Cross of Calvary. The Apostle John
describes and identifies these false prophets in his first
epistle (read I John 4:1-3):

> Beloved, believe not every spirit, but try the spirits
> whether they are of God: because *many false prophets*
> are gone out into the world. Hereby know ye the Spirit of
> God: Every spirit that confesseth that Jesus Christ is come
> in the flesh is of God: And every spirit that confesseth not
> that Jesus Christ is come in the flesh is not of God.

Solemn words are these. John says, "Jesus Christ is come in the flesh." The word "Jesus" means "Jehovah Saviour." It comes from two Hebrew words, *Jehovah* and *Hoshea*. By contraction we get "Joshua." The Greek form of the Hebrew word *Joshua* is "Jesus." The word "Christ" is a translation of the Hebrew word *Messiah*, meaning "the Anointed One." "Jesus Christ," therefore, means "God the Saviour," "the Anointed One." According to John, anyone who does not confess that God became man is a false prophet. God was manifest in the flesh. The Word became flesh. According to the Word of God, this is the test whereby to try the spirits, whether or not they be of God. Everyone who does not confess that Jesus Christ was God manifest in the flesh is not of God. When we think of the teaching of modern, philosophical theology, we understand what Jesus was speaking about. What confusion and what denial of the cardinal truths of the Word of God we see! This preaching of a diluted, ex-sanguinated, eviscerated, decapitated and emasculated Gospel and the flattery of pretty words and high-sounding shibboleths has led multitudes astray. Jude describes these false prophets thus:

> Murmurers, complainers, walking after their own lusts; and their mouth speaketh great swelling words, having men's persons in admiration because of advantage (Jude 16).

If ever we Christians have prayed, it should be today that we may be given the spirit of discernment lest we be led away by the error of the wicked and their appealing but false gospel, of which Paul said:

> If any man preach any other gospel unto you than that ye have received, let him be accursed (Gal. 1:9).

7. *INCREASE OF INIQUITY*
8. *APOSTASY*

These two signs are related. They are the abounding of iniquity and the "growing cold" of many who before this time were warm with love. Need we comment on this seventh sign? Hardly, when we consider the fact that the crime bill of the nation is estimated at sixteen billion dollars annually. Our daily papers are the best commentaries on these words of the Lord Jesus and coincident with this is the lukewarmness of the Church. From earnest preachers in every quarter comes the cry that a lukewarmness and indifference are creeping over God's people. Preaching does not seem to touch them. Our Lord spoke of these things nineteen hundred years ago as signs of His soon return.

9. *UNIVERSAL GOSPEL PREACHING*

Jesus speaks of the last sign in these words: "This gospel of the kingdom shall be preached in all the world for a witness unto all nations; and then shall the end come." I realize that this will be fulfilled *after* the Rapture, but it is beginning to be fulfilled *before* the Rapture. For the first time in history it is possible to reach the whole world with the Gospel. The radio is able to send that message to every nook and corner of the globe. If we could supply everyone with a receiving set and then preach in his language we could fulfill these words of the Lord Jesus to the letter. During the Tribulation the Gospel will be brought to *all* men by the converted 144,000 of Israel; it will be accomplished largely by the "hearing of the ear" — by means of the radio. Thus we see that these nine signs enumerated by Jesus in Matthew 24 are in the process of fulfillment.

I know that some will raise the objection that all these things have happened before. There have always been false christs and false prophets. There have always been wars, rumors of wars, famines, pestilences, earthquakes, anti-Semitism and wickedness. Yes, that is indeed true. However, all of these signs have never been present at the same time. In these days in which we are living *all* the signs are present simultaneously. This has never before happened and surely the words of Jesus become richly significant: "When these things begin to come to pass." In Luke 21:28 we read:

> And when these things begin to come to pass, then look up, and lift up your heads; for your redemption draweth nigh.

These things will not be fulfilled until after the believers are raptured, but our Lord emphasizes that when they *begin* to come to pass, we are to look up. The days spoken of are upon us, and what a blessing it is to bring this message of hope to a hopeless world! Soon the Lord will come. For the first time in history *all* these things are *beginning* at the same time. For the first time in history we can begin to preach the Gospel to all nations by means of the radio. For the first time in history earthquakes are occurring in divers places. Soon He who said He would come will come and will not tarry.

THE TWOFOLD COMING OF CHRIST

> Behold, I come as a thief. Blessed is he that watcheth, and keepeth his garments, lest he walk naked, and they see his shame (Rev. 16:15).
>
> Behold, he cometh with clouds; and every eye shall see him, and they also which pierced him: and all kindreds of the earth shall wail because of him (Rev. 1:7).

Both of these passages refer to the coming again of the Lord Jesus Christ. Yet in the one His coming is described as secret and sudden like that of a thief in the dead of night, unobserved except by those for whom He comes. He disappears again before the rest of the people are aware of His visit. The Lord says, "Behold, I come as a thief." In the other event He is described as coming publicly. "He cometh with clouds; and *every* eye shall see him." Both of these passages refer to the second coming of Christ, but to two distinct phases of that second coming.

All Christians believe in the coming again of Jesus. To reject His coming again is to reject His Word, and the record which God has given concerning His Son. That record concerns His second coming as well as His first.

All Christians, however, are not agreed as to the details of His coming again. There are some who believe that the world will get better and better until, through the influence of the Gospel, education, better understanding among the nations, inventions, science, legislation and reformation, the world will cease its warfare and strife and finally usher in a golden age of peace. After this golden age of peace the Lord will come back to judge the world. People who believe this are called "Postmillennarians" because they "postpone" the coming of the Lord until after the Millennium.

There are also those who deny that there will be a Millennium. They teach that the world will continue to become worse and worse until the end of time. Then the Lord will come to judge the earth and usher in eternity. These people are "Amillennarians," meaning *"No* Millennium."

Finally, there are those who interpret the Bible literally. These maintain that the Lord will come at any time. They believe the Bible teaches that the world will become more and more wicked as the end of this age approaches, that the Church will wax cold and apostate, that wars will increase, hatred and iniquity shall abound and then, when everything is black and dark for the world, the "Lord himself shall descend from heaven with a shout, with the voice of the archangel, and with the trump of God: and the dead in Christ shall rise first: then we which are alive and remain shall be caught up together with them in the clouds to meet the Lord in the air" (I Thess. 4:16-17). This we call the "Rapture" of the Church, which is the secret sudden coming of Christ for His own. Immediately after the Church is raptured, the Antichrist will be revealed, the time of the world's greatest sorrow and anguish will begin and for seven years the Tribulation will last, when the world will experience the greatest period of sorrow, warfare, bloodshed and destruction in its history. So intense will be that holocaust that unless those days are shortened no flesh shall be saved. During this period of tribulation on earth the Church will be with the Lord in the air. Then, at the close of this brief but intense period of tribulation, the Lord will come again publicly on the clouds of heaven with His glorified Church which was caught away before the Tribulation. He shall descend with her until His feet stand on the Mount of Olives from which He ascended — after His first coming — and at the touch of His omnipotent feet the mountain will split wide open, causing a valley to be formed from east to west from the Mediterranean Sea to the Dead Sea, through which the waters of the ocean will rush, forming the greatest inland seaport in the world, with Jerusalem on its banks as the greatest city in the world. The Lord will then destroy His enemies and the enemies of Israel. He will set up His kingdom on the throne of David and reign over the earth for one thousand blessed years. Those who believe this are called "Premillennarians" because they believe the Word of God concerning the coming again of Christ to set up His kingdom *before* the Millennium. After the Millennium will come the end of the world, when God shall sit on the Great White Throne and the wicked dead will be judged and cast into the Lake of Fire. The redeemed shall dwell with Him forever in a new and rejuvenated heaven and earth, where there will be no sorrow, death nor pain but everlasting peace and perfect contentment and blessing with our reunited loved ones and Jesus Christ forever and ever.

THE TWO PHASES OF CHRIST'S COMING AGAIN

There are two phases of His coming again. The one is *before* the Tribulation, when Christ comes *for* His Church, to take her *out* of the earth so that she will escape the awful blood bath of the day of the Lord. This first aspect is part of Christ's second coming called the "blessed hope" in Titus. It is with this part that we shall deal particularly.

> For the grace of God that bringeth salvation hath appeared to all men, teaching us that, denying ungodliness and worldly lusts, we should live soberly, righteously, and godly, in this present world; *looking for that blessed hope* (Titus 2:11-13).

It is the blessed hope for the believer, the hope of deliverance from the increase of iniquity in the world, the spreading specter of universal war and hatred, and the coming crash of civilization, but more even than that, it is the blessed hope of being forever with the Lord. The Church will witness this fearful time of tribulation from heaven but will have no part in it on the earth. In Luke 21 we have a detailed description of that awful day of tribulation. After that description the Lord says, in Luke 21:36:

> Watch ye therefore, and pray always, that ye may be accounted worthy to escape all these things that shall come to pass, and to stand before the Son of man.

There will be some who will "escape *all* these things . . . and to stand before the Son of man." These are they who "watch and pray" — the Church which He purchased with His own blood.

In Revelation, John, writing to the church of Philadelphia (the true portion of the apostate Church of the last days), says:

> Because thou hast kept the word of my patience, I also will keep thee from the hour of temptation, which shall come upon all the world, to try them that dwell upon the earth (Rev. 3:10).

ENOCH AND LOT

Jesus, in speaking of the last days, uses two figures from history: the Flood and the destruction of Sodom. Of the first He says, "As the days of Noah were, so shall also the coming of the Son of man be." Of the second He says, "Likewise also as it was in the days of Lot . . . even thus shall it be in the day when the Son of man is revealed." Both were times of terrible judgment. These are the two greatest catastrophies in history. Jesus uses them as figures of the coming greater judgment of the Tribulation. However, in each case someone was taken out before the judgment came. Enoch was translated *before* the Flood. Lot was taken out *before* Sodom was destroyed. Enoch was a godly man who walked with God. Lot was a carnal man, and yet, according to II Peter 2:7 he was a righteous man.

> And delivered just Lot, vexed with the filthy conversation of the wicked: (for that righteous man dwelling among them, in seeing, and hearing, vexed his righteous soul from day to day with their unlawful deeds;) the Lord knoweth how to deliver the godly out of temptations [trials], and to reserve the unjust unto the day of judgment to be punished (II Peter 2:7-9).

Enoch, a spiritual man, was translated to bliss and a reward. Lot, the carnal man, was delivered but to be disgraced. He lost his reward and was judged by losing his all.

There are two kinds of believers. Some are spiritual. Others are carnal or worldly. When the Lord comes all believers shall be taken out before the judgment falls. Some, like Enoch, shall be given an "abundant" entrance and shall receive a reward (I Cor. 3); others, like Lot, shall be saved, "yet so as by fire" (I Cor. 3). Some, like Enoch, shall have confidence at His appearing, and others, like Lot, shall be "ashamed before him at his coming" (I John 2:28). Some, like Enoch, shall receive a "full reward," and others, like Lot, will lose their reward (II John 8). Some, like Enoch, shall be given dominion over ten or five cities, whereas others, like Lot, shall be rebuked when the King returns (Luke 19).

THE STAR AND THE SUN

The deliverances of Enoch and Lot were sudden and quick. This illustrates the "thief aspect" of the Lord's coming before the judgment falls upon the rest of the world. When the judgment falls and the Lord comes in His glorious appearing, "every eye" shall see Him. The Lord's coming is represented as the rising of the Morning Star (Mal. 4). It is also spoken of as "lightning" which shines from one end of heaven to the other. The morning star appears at the darkest part of the night. It rises above the horizon suddenly just before the blackest part of the night. It is seen and greeted only by a few who are watching for it. The rest of the world is asleep. Only astronomers and heaven-gazers see the morning star. The sun, on the contrary, floods the whole world with light and awakens all nature. To the Church the coming of Christ is like the rising of the morning star. He speaks in Revelation 2:26 to the faithful ones in Thyatira as follows:

> And he that overcometh, and keepeth my works unto the end, to him will I give power over the nations: and he shall rule them with a rod of iron; as the vessels of a potter shall they be broken to shivers: even as I received of my Father. And I will give him the morning star.

Jesus Christ is the Morning Star of the believer. When He appears He will take His bride (the Church) home while the world is fast asleep. Then will follow the darkest brief period of tribulation between the appearing of the morning star and the sunrise. After this dark tribulation period the Sun of Righteousness will appear. This was promised through Malachi to Israel. After that terrible tribulation, when the Jews have endured the fires of their greatest testing and have acknowledged their Messiah, He will suddenly come to His temple in the glory of His second coming. Like the sun He will flood the world with the light of His glory, purify the earth with judgment, and bring in the glorious millennial reign. Israel shall be gathered safely in the land of Palestine and the nations shall be at peace, while the Church will reign with Christ over the earth. His coming will be "star rise then sunrise." Between these two will be the day of judgment of our Lord.

THE THIEF IS NEAR

How near this great day is we do not know, but we know that it is very near. One thing is certain: we are nearer that day now than we have ever been. Soon the Lord shall come as a thief in the night. There are many suggestions in this figure of the thief. It is for this reason that the coming of the Lord for His Church before the Tribulation is called in the Scripture a coming "as a thief." For the true believer, however, Christ's coming will not be like that of a thief. This applies only to those who know Him not. Paul in writing to the Thessalonian Christians, says:

> But ye, brethren, are not in darkness, that that day should overtake you as a thief. Ye are all the children of light, and the children of the day: we are not of the night, nor of darkness. Therefore let us not sleep, as do others; but let us watch and be sober (I Thess. 5:4-6).

Christians, are you watching for that day? Are you ready? Do not let that day "overtake you as a thief" and find you unprepared to meet Him. Many Christians are "waiting" for Him but they are not "watching." They believe He is coming but they are not concerned about it. A man may *wait* and still not be ready. To be ready one must *watch.* A man in a railroad station may be waiting for the train and fall fast asleep, but the man who is watching for the train will be wide awake. O Christian, if you knew how near that day really was, how it would stir you to action! How you would cease to live for this old world, and set your affections on things above. I am sure that many of you would catch a vision of the need for getting the Gospel out in the few days we have left. You would do your utmost to get this word of loving warning out. Christian, awake. He is at the very door!

HOW THE THIEF COMES

The figure of a thief suggests many things about the coming of the Lord. I will enumerate a few:

1. He comes at the darkest part of the night.
2. He comes quietly and unobserved by sleepers.
3. He comes to snatch something.
4. He is after jewels and gold and pearls.
5. He is not interested in things of no value.
6. He has come and gone before others are aware of it.
7. He leaves the house greatly impoverished but himself greatly enriched.

Jesus said, "Behold, I come as a thief." He will come at a dark period of the world's night. Has it ever been darker than today? Kingdoms are tottering and falling. Violence is rampant in the world, and the devil and his dictators are on the loose. Immorality, crime, apostasy and hate are everywhere. Yes, it is dark, but a darker time is yet to come. Just before the darkest hour the thief will come. We can hear His soft tread if we are wide awake, listening, watching believers. Soon He will catch us away and then the darkest period of history will come.

The thief comes to snatch away that which has value. He is after the pearl of great price (Matt. 13). That pearl is the Church. It may be somewhat tarnished, and I fear it is, but He will snatch it and thoroughly cleanse it before He comes back in the brightness of glory, wearing His precious pearl that will then be without spot or blemish. The pearl (or anything of great value) has worth only because of its purchase price. When Jesus comes like a thief He will take only those who have value by reason of the fact that they were purchased by His blood. All others will be left behind.

The thief does not take worthless things. He does not bother with the wastebasket or the rubbish pile. He leaves these behind. Reader, heed this: if you are not saved — born again by His Spirit and washed in His blood — you are worthless in His sight. You will be left behind to face the wrath of God. You will be destroyed in that "day of the Lord."

Are you ready for that day? It may come very soon, and then for those who have heard the Word and rejected it, it will be forever too late. While it is true that multitudes will be saved after the Church is taken out and that these multitudes shall be from every tribe and tongue and nation, it is true also that these multitudes will be those who have not heard the Gospel of the grace of God as you have. Are you ready? As surely as the Lord Jesus came the first time He will come again the second time.

Reader, are you ready? Accept the Lord Jesus as your Saviour and you will not need to meet Him as your Judge.

THAT BLESSED HOPE

> But I would not have you to be ignorant, brethren, concerning them which are asleep, that ye sorrow not, even as others which have no hope. For if we believe that Jesus died and rose again, even so them also which sleep in Jesus will God bring with him. For this we say unto you by the word of the Lord, that we which are alive and remain unto the coming of the Lord shall not prevent them which are asleep. For the Lord himself shall descend from heaven with a shout, with the voice of the archangel, and with the trump of God: and the dead in Christ shall rise first: then we which are alive and remain shall be caught up together with them in the clouds, to meet the Lord in the air: and so shall we ever be with the Lord. Wherefore comfort one another with these words (I Thess. 4:13-18).

This is probably the best known passage in the New Testament setting forth the event which is called "that blessed hope." It is the coming of the Lord Jesus Christ for His Church at the close of this present dispensation — just before the breaking of that day of the earth's greatest testing and trial, the Tribulation. This revelation is all the more precious because it occurs in one of Paul's earliest (if not the very first) letters. This letter, written to the Thessalonian church, a church which Paul established on his second missionary journey, reveals to us how fervently Paul looked for the return of the Lord Jesus Christ. We shall divide the passage into five parts. These divisions are as follows:

1. The occasion for the epistle (vs. 13).
2. The condition of the blessed hope (vs. 14).
3. The authority of the revelation (vs. 15).
4. The order of the blessed hope (vss. 16-17).
5. The result of His coming (vs. 18).

THE OCCASION

Some years prior to the writing of this letter to the Thessalonians, Paul had spent two weeks at Thessalonica and faithfully preached the Gospel. He had not failed to include in this preaching the blessed truth of the imminent return of the Lord Jesus Christ. He had comforted the Christians at Thessalonica with the assurance that the trials and tribulations of these early Christians should not alarm them, for the Lord would return and take them unto Himself very shortly and set up His glorious kingdom. As these testings and trials came they took heart and said, "It will not last forever; soon the Lord will come and take us out to reign with Him." Then something very disturbing happened. Some of their number became ill and died. As they carried them away, doubts and fears arose in their hearts. Had not Paul told them that the Lord was coming, and that when He came they would enter the kingdom with Him? What about these who had died? You can see that they, like many today, knew nothing of the first resurrection. They believed in a post-millennial, general resurrection — that when the Lord set up His millennial kingdom the dead would not share in this glory, since they were not to be resurrected until *after* that glorious age. These early Christians were sad, as every one is who knows not the truth of the "blessed hope." Paul hears of their troubles and doubts. He immediately writes this epistle to correct their misunderstanding of the coming of the Lord. He reveals to them that the dead in Christ will not be denied the privilege of the glorious millennial reign with Christ, since they will be raised when He comes to set up the kingdom.

THE CONDITION

Before giving the details of this coming Paul lays down the one condition upon which we may appropriate this blessed hope to ourselves, when he says:

> For if we believe that Jesus died and rose again, even so them also which sleep in Jesus will God bring with him.

The one condition of salvation is faith in the death and the Resurrection of Jesus Christ. Only those who have received Him and have confessed with their mouths the Lord Jesus and believed in their hearts "that God hath raised him from the dead" can appropriate the comfort of this "blessed hope." Salvation is not by works, or goodness, or human effort, but entirely by faith. The word translated "if" in verse 14 may also be translated "since." The context determines which should be used and we may read it as follows: "For [*since*] we have believed that Jesus died and rose again, even so them also which sleep in Jesus will God bring with him." One of these days the Lord Jesus is coming again, and then only those who have trusted Him and accepted Him as their Saviour will rise to meet Him in the air. All the rest, no matter what their moral or religious merits may be, will be left behind to face the wrath of God.

All those who have come to Christ by faith are encouraged by the truth which follows. Paul is telling these Thessalonian believers that the dead in Christ — the ones who had gone on before — will not be denied the blessing of that event. He says, "Even so them also which sleep in Jesus will God bring with him." The expression "asleep in Jesus" is incorrect. In the Bible, believers are never said to be "in Jesus" except in this one instance. Believers

are said to be "in Christ." In II Corinthians 5:17 we read,
"If any man be *in Christ*." In this same chapter we are
told that the "dead *in Christ*" shall rise first. The error
lies in a mistranslation. The Greek word *dia*, here translated "in," should have been translated "by means of."
Thus the verse reads "Even so them also which sleep will
God [*by means of* Jesus] bring with him." Everyone who
is "in Christ" will be "with Christ" when He comes.

THE AUTHORITY

Next Paul gives the authority on which he is making
this revelation:

> . . . for this we say unto you by the word of the Lord.

It is a very significant fact that whenever the coming of
Christ is mentioned in the Bible, God always accompanies
or precedes the statement with the warning not to tamper
with this truth. In the Old Testament the prophetic
portions are almost invariably introduced by such expressions as "thus saith the Lord," "hear the word of the
Lord" or other expressions. The Lord knew that the truth
of prophecy and the coming again of Christ would be
scoffed at by the unbelievers, as well as tragically ignored
by the host of professing Christians. Because of this,
almost invariably the Spirit adds a warning to remind us
of the seriousness of tampering with the truth of the
Lord's return. Note that Paul says, "For this we say unto
you by the word of the Lord." In other words, if you
reject this revelation you are not rejecting the word of
man but the "word of the Lord." Yet, in spite of all these
warnings, how much rejection of this truth there is today.
Even among orthodox believers one cannot find another
doctrine on which there has been greater difference of
opinion than that concerning the truth of the coming
again of Christ and the Millennium. We have the "Post-
millennarian," the "Amillennarian," the "Premillennarian,"
the "pre-Tribulation Rapturist," the "post-Tribulation

Rapturist," the "mid-Tribulation Rapturist" and the "Partial Rapturist." How is a man going to know the truth when apparently sincere and able men are found among all of these groups? There is only one answer and that is to go, personally and directly, to the Scriptures and then receive and accept what they have to say concerning this great truth. Let us see what Paul reveals in the remainder of this passage:

THE ORDER

After having warned us not to tamper with this revelation, Paul gives the order of the events at the coming of Christ for His Church:

1. The Lord Himself will descend from heaven.
2. The Lord will shout.
3. The Lord will allow the archangel to speak.
4. He will blow a trumpet.
5. The dead in Christ will rise first.
6. The living believers will join the raised ones.
7. They will be reunited.
8. Then they will rise into the air.
9. They will meet the Lord.
10. They will remain ever with Him.

Ten definite events will occur, according to this passage.

There is a certain, sweet comfort in the expression "the Lord himself." "The Lord himself shall descend from heaven with a shout." The same Lord who nineteen hundred years ago went into heaven to prepare a place for us will come again. Does not every believer's heart quicken its beat at those words? The "Lord himself"; the One whom, "having not seen, [we] love"; the precious, blessed Lord who left heaven's glories and laid aside the form of God and took upon Himself our human nature to redeem us from the pit of hell and to lift us into sonship with God — He will come again. Soon we will see the same Jesus who walked the weary way to Calvary, bearing the

Cross on which we should have died; the same Jesus who
hung on that Cross for six dread hours, with all the
weight of a world's guilt laid upon Him and the infinite
wrath of God bursting upon Him for our sin, until the
very sun, which He had created, could not bear to behold
the sight any longer, and as the Light of the World
slipped into the darkness of death, the sun hid its face,
God drew the shutters of heaven, blew out the Light of
the World and turned His back upon His own Son until
He cried out in the inexpressible agony of His soul, "My
God, my God, why hast thou forsaken me?" There He
bore our sin and shame — the sin that hid God's face from
us — the sin that deserved eternal death. He bore it there.
He paid it there for *me* — for *you*. Now we are redeemed
and saved from hell and damnation because He loved us
so.

It was this same Jesus who found me when I was lost
and condemned in sin, hating God, reviling His Word,
cursing His Son, murdering the Prince of Life. It was
He who loved me enough to take my guilt and to make it
His responsibility; to save me and to make me a son of
God; to put a song in my heart, a testimony on my lips
and the assurance of eternal life in my soul. That same
Lord Himself will descend from heaven one of these days
— that precious, adorable Lord — my Lord and my God
— my Saviour and my King. I shall look upon Him. I
shall see the *Lord Himself*. O friend, that is for you, too,
if you have believed on Him. Can you begin to imagine
the thrill that will sweep over us when for the first time
we behold Him, see Him, the One who died for us to save
our poor, hell-bound, sin-smitten souls from eternal destruction? Yes, the Lord Himself will descend.

Notice that while we ascend — the Lord descends.
However, He does not come to the earth at this stage of
His coming. It is definitely stated that we shall meet
Him in the air. He descends and we ascend, but we meet

above the earth. It is important to note this carefully, as there is a time when the Lord shall descend to the earth.

The Prophet Zechariah tells us that when the Lord descends to the earth, "his feet shall stand . . . upon the mount of Olives." He will march into Jerusalem with His saints, who have previously ascended in the Rapture, to meet Him in the air. In this prophecy we are told about the second stage of the coming of the Lord. It describes the actual coming again of the Lord Jesus to the earth — with His saints.

The first phase of this coming is the "Thief Aspect" and the other is the "Judgment Aspect" of the coming again of our Lord.

In Titus 2:13 we read, "Looking for that blessed hope, and the glorious appearing of the great God and our Saviour Jesus Christ." The "Blessed Hope" is His coming in the air for His saints; His glorious appearing is His coming with His saints to the earth. Between these two, we have the time spoken of as "the day of the Lord" — the seven years of judgment and tribulation.

HE IS COMING WITH A SHOUT

Paul says, "The Lord shall descend from heaven with a shout." He is now in heaven. He has been there for nineteen hundred years waiting for the time of His coming again. He is there to look after our interests and prepare a place for us. In the meantime, through the Holy Spirit, He is gathering out His bride here upon the earth. When the number determined for that bride has been brought in, through the preaching of the Gospel and the work of the Holy Spirit, the Lord Himself will come again.

He will come with a shout. It will be the shout of the omnipotent Christ of God. In Revelation 1, John pictures Him as the one with head and hair as white as snow, with feet like burnished brass, with a priestly robe and a golden girdle, with eyes like a flame of fire and a voice like the sound of many waters. It will be the same voice that brought into being the heavens and the earth at the beginning of creation. By the word of the Lord were the heavens made and the earth. It was His voice that spoke on Sinai and shook the earth and heavens. It was His voice that said to a dead man in a tomb, "Lazarus, come forth." It was His voice that said to the angry waves of the sea, "Peace, be still," and the hurricane heard that voice, fell on its face on the glassy, watery floor, and came and licked its Master's hand. It was this same voice that cried at that zero hour of all eternity, as He hung on the Cross, "It is finished." At that voice the veil of the Temple was rent in twain, the earth quaked, the rocks rent, the graves of many of the saints were opened and they that slept arose. This same voice will again be heard. How soon we do not know. When that time comes, the graves once more will be opened and all those that sleep in Christ will come forth to be raptured with the changed, living believers to meet the Lord in the air.

The Lord shall descend from heaven with a shout. That shout will be heard only by believers, either dead or alive. None of the wicked dead will hear it. They shall remain in their graves. Nor will any of the unbelieving living hear that shout. It may be that they will know something has happened because every true Christian will suddenly be gone, but the shout will be heard only by those who are the Lord's. If you ask, "How can some hear and not others?" we have the answer. The radio has made it possible for sounds to be heard by some and not by others. You know the reason, of course. Some are tuned in to the right wave length, whereas others are tuned in to other wave lengths. Thus it will be at the coming of the Lord. Only those who are tuned to Station "BLOOD" will hear that shout. Only those who are tuned to the wave length of heaven will hear that call, "Come up hither." The others will be tuned to earth and will be unaware of that shout.

O friend, are you under the blood? Is your heart tuned by faith to the voice of God? If it is, when He comes you will be caught up. If not, you will be left behind to face the wrath of God. Prepare to meet thy God. The Lord shall descend from heaven with a shout and every believer will be caught away to meet the Lord.

Believe on the Lord Jesus Christ, and thou shalt be saved.

THE ARCHANGEL

Accompanying the Lord Jesus Christ, as He descends from the sky, will be the "archangel." There are multitudes of angels and we know that there are angels of different rank and order. Michael, one of the archangels, was the angel whose duty it was to watch over the children of Israel. The few times that he is mentioned in the Scriptures he is always associated with the deliverance of the Israelites. Gabriel seems to be the angel to whom was entrusted the conveying of important messages from God to men — while the archangel Michael's ministry seems to be limited to God's ancient people Israel. Daniel tells us in the twelfth chapter of the book of Daniel:

> And at that time shall Michael stand up, the great prince which standeth for the children of thy people: and there shall be a time of trouble, such as never was since there was a nation even to that same time: and at that time thy people shall be delivered, every one that shall be found written in the book (Dan. 12:1).

Note the expression "children of thy people" (Daniel's people). In every other passage where Michael the archangel is mentioned he is associated with the deliverance of the nation of Israel. How significant, then, that when the Lord shouts from the air to call His bride home, that event should be accompanied by the voice of the archangel. The taking out of the Church is also the signal for the beginning of the day of Jacob's trouble. For twenty-five hundred years Israel, as a nation, has been scattered among all other nations and for nineteen hundred years the Jews have had no land to call their own. Jerusalem has been under the heel of their enemies. The Bible tells us that in that period between the Rapture of the Church and the setting up of the millennial kingdom there will be a time of "tribulation" and "trouble" such as the world has never seen and never will see again. This time is particularly called the "time of Jacob's trouble." In that day anti-Semitism will reach an all-time high — its very peak, in fact. The enemies of the Lord and of His people, according to the flesh, under the leadership of the Antichrist, will make one final attempt to annihilate and banish Israel from the earth forever. The work that Pharaoh began in Egypt and which has been carried forth by the nations since will then reach its climax. But the same God who raised up a Moses and delivered His people from Egypt — the same God who has preserved this nation through all the succeeding centuries and millenniums — is still the same covenant-keeping God and will once more deliver them in that day of Jacob's trouble. It seemed hopeless in the days of Pharaoh, but God was able. It has seemed hopeless many times since, but always God has delivered.

When Jesus calls the Church, the greatest day of sorrow Israel has even seen or known will begin, but the appearance of the archangel, with the Lord, is God's guarantee and assurance that they will not be utterly destroyed but rather will be delivered and returned to their own land of Palestine. Then all the covenant promises of God will be completely fulfilled.

THREE CLASSES OF PEOPLE

According to I Corinthians 10:32 there are three groups of people in the world today. Paul says in this verse:

> Give none offence, neither to the Jews, nor to the Gentiles, nor to the church of God.

All men on the earth belong to one of these three classes. The Jew is one who is the natural descendant of

Abraham, through Isaac and Jacob. The Gentile is one who is not a descendant of Abraham. The Church is the body of believers, either Jew or Gentile, who have trusted in the finished work of Christ, who have been born by the Spirit and are, therefore, saved — heirs of eternal life through His Name. You are either a member of the first, the second or the third group — for there are no others. Either you are a Jew, a Gentile or a Christian. At the time of the coming of the Lord these three classes will be on the earth, and at His coming, He will have a message for each of these groups. To the Church, He will shout from the air, "Rise up, my love, my fair one, and come away. For, lo, the winter is past, the rain is over and gone; the flowers appear on the earth; the time of the singing of birds is come" (Cant. 2:10-12). To the nation of Israel the archangel will utter this message: "Behold, I will take the children of Israel from among the heathen, whither they be gone, and will gather them on every side, and bring them into their own land: and I will make them one nation in the land upon the mountains of Israel . . . And they shall dwell in the land that I have given unto Jacob my servant . . . I will make a covenant of peace with them; it shall be an everlasting covenant with them . . . My tabernacle also shall be with them: yea, I will be their God, and they shall be my people" (Ezek. 37).

THE TRUMP

Just as the coming of the Lord has a message for the Church and for Israel, so, too, it has a message for the Gentile nations, who have rejected the Christ and persecuted His people. The text says, "The Lord himself shall descend from heaven with a shout, the voice of the archangel, and with the *Trump of God*." The trumpet in Scripture had two meanings (in the economy of Israel). When the trumpet was blown once it meant that the Israelites should prepare to march. When the trumpet was blown twice, it was a call to war. Here in I Thessalonians 4, we have both meanings. The trump will call God's people to march, and we shall be caught up to meet Him. It will also be the signal for the nations to prepare for war, for after the Church is taken out the nations will assemble themselves and the end will come in the battle of Armageddon, resulting in the utter defeat of the enemies of the Lord. This call to war is given in Joel in very clear terms:

> Blow ye the trumpet in Zion, and sound an alarm in my holy mountain: let all the inhabitants of the land tremble: for the day of the Lord cometh, for it is nigh at hand . . . The Lord shall utter his voice before his army: for his camp is very great (Joel 2:1, 11).
> Proclaim ye this among the Gentiles; Prepare war, wake up the mighty men, let all the men of war draw near; let them come up: beat your plowshares into swords, and your pruninghooks into spears: let the weak say, I am strong. Assemble yourselves, and come all ye heathen, and gather yourselves together round about: thither cause thy mighty ones to come down, O Lord. Let the heathen be wakened, and come up to the valley of Jehoshaphat: for there will I sit to judge all the heathen round about (Joel 3:9-12).

The coming of the Lord will be the signal that marshals the armies of the world for the last great and final conflict, which will result in a complete victory for Christ and the establishment of His long promised millennial kingdom. Then the prayer which has ascended from millions of hearts for nineteen centuries will finally be answered:

> Thy kingdom come. Thy will be done in earth, as it is in heaven.

THE RESURRECTION

The coming of the Lord will affect all the inhabitants of the earth. The Church will be "caught away"; Israel will be put through the "fiery furnace of tribulation" but finally gloriously delivered by the archangel; and the nations will be judged and brought into subjection.

Then Paul gives the order of the events as they relate to the Church (I Thess. 4:16, 17):

> For the Lord himself shall descend from heaven with a
> shout, with the voice of the archangel, and with the trump
> of God: and the dead in Christ shall rise first: then we
> which are alive and remain shall be caught up together with
> them in the clouds, to meet the Lord in the air.

The dead in Christ shall rise first. Certainly this statement alone is enough to refute the unscriptural theory held by so much of Christendom that "all the dead will rise simultaneously" at the general resurrection at the last day. Jesus says, through Paul, "The dead in Christ shall rise *first*." This implies that the dead out of Christ will rise later. Surely if the dead "in Christ" are to rise first, the others will rise last. So it is. At the coming of the Lord Jesus only those who have died in the faith will rise in their glorified bodies. John tells us in Revelation 20 that the "wicked dead" will not be raised until *after* the thousand years — then to be judged at the Great White Throne. The dead in Christ, however, will live and reign with Christ for a thousand years before that time and so they must of necessity be raised before the Kingdom Age. Scripture plainly states:

> But the rest of the dead lived not again until the
> thousand years were finished (Rev. 20:5).

Immediately after the resurrection of the "saved" dead, the living believers will be changed. They shall pass from mortality to immortality. In a moment our bodies will be changed into the likeness of His glorious body. We will have immortal, spiritual, painless, perfect, eternal, deathless bodies. This will occur at the coming of Christ, for the Apostle Paul says:

> For our conversation is in heaven; from whence also we
> look for the Saviour, the Lord Jesus Christ: who shall
> change our vile body, that it may be fashioned like unto his
> glorious body, according to the working whereby he is able
> even to subdue all things unto himself (Phil. 3:20-21).

The dead in Christ shall rise first, then we which are alive and remain shall be caught up together with them. In I Corinthians 15:51-53 we read:

> Behold, I shew you a mystery; We shall not all sleep, but we shall all be changed, in a moment, in the twinkling of an eye, at the last trump: for the trumpet shall sound, and the dead shall be raised incorruptible, and we shall be changed. For this corruptible [the dead] must put on incorruption, and this mortal [the living] must put on immortality.

Notice the order. First, the dead shall be raised incorruptible, and then we shall be changed.

Jesus teaches the same truth in John 11. You recall that after Lazarus had died Jesus was met by Martha before He came to the tomb, and she said, "Lord, if thou hadst been here, my brother had not died." Jesus answered, "Thy brother shall rise again." Martha answered, "I know that he shall rise again in the resurrection at the last day." Martha knew nothing of the first resurrection. She held the common notion that there would be only one general resurrection at the last day. Then Jesus revealed to her the comforting truth of the first resurrection of the saved before the kingdom, at the coming of the Lord for His Church:

> Jesus said unto her, I am the resurrection, and the life; he that believeth in me, though he were dead, yet shall he live (John 11:25).

This speaks of the resurrection of the dead believers. "He that believeth in me, though he were dead, yet shall he live," said Jesus. Then He added:

> And whosoever liveth [is alive when that occurs] and believeth in me shall never die (John 11:26).

The dead in Christ shall rise first; then we which are alive shall be changed without dying. "He that believeth in me, though he were dead, yet shall he live: and whosoever liveth and believeth in me shall never die."

THE MEETING IN THE AIR

Every unbeliever will be left behind. The unsaved dead will remain in their graves and their souls will be in torment, not to be raised until a thousand years later. The living unbelievers will remain on the earth to face the wrath of God, and if not subsequently saved they will face death in that awful day only to join the others who are lost until the last resurrection of the damned at the end of time and at the Great White Throne.

But the saved (resurrected and changed) will then begin their upward translation. Paul says, "We shall be caught up together *with them to meet* the Lord in the air." Before we meet Jesus at His coming we will be reunited with our loved ones who have gone on before. All of us have loved ones for whom we yearn and whom we miss much. We have mothers, fathers, brothers and sisters over yonder and sometimes we get homesick to see them. Do you remember the day that little flaxen-haired blue-eyed darling breathed her last earthly breath and the Lord took her away from this vile wicked world to be with Him? What tears you have wept, and how you long to see her again. Listen, friend, if you are a believer you will see that darling again, for the "dead in Christ shall rise first: then we which are alive and remain shall be caught up *together with them* . . . to meet the Lord in the air."

"Together with them . . . to meet the Lord." That means that before we are caught up to meet Jesus we will be brought together and reunited with our loved ones. We will rise to meet Him not only as individuals but as reunited groups. We will be brought together and there will be a quick fond greeting of our loved ones and then together we will be caught up. When we meet Jesus we will meet Him together with our saved families. How the thought thrills our souls! While we long to see the Lord Jesus who died for us, we also long to see the dear ones gone on before. I have a mother up there, a father, a sister, a brother and a host of other dear ones and friends. Before I am caught up to meet Him I will meet Mother and Father and brother and sister. There will be one rapturous moment of fond greeting and then we will be caught up together with them to meet the Lord in the air.

> Friends will be there I have loved long ago;
> Joy like a river around me will flow;
> Yet, just a smile from my Saviour, I know,
> Will thro' the ages be glory for me.

Then Paul says, "And so shall we ever be with the Lord." We will be perfect in His presence. There will be no more suffering, pain or sickness; no more weeping, distress, disappointment or struggle; no more stumbling, failing and falling; no more sinning; no more slipping. With new bodies — immortal, sinless, painless — we shall ever enjoy the eternal glories of His presence and His kingdom.

This is the "blessed hope." This is the one bright spot in a dark world. This is the glad anticipation of the believer who trusts in Christ. The war clouds may loom darker and blacker. The roar of cannon may roll; the boom of guns may make the earth tremble; the nations may assemble for war; civilization may totter on the brink of destruction and man may seek to annihilate himself, but to those who know the truth of "that blessed hope" these things are but the footsteps of the coming King, and we lift up our heads for our "redemption draweth nigh."

CHAPTER TWO

That Blessed Hope

I. THE RAPTURE OF THE CHURCH

> Let not your heart be troubled: ye believe in God, believe also in me. In my Father's house are many mansions: if it were not so, I would have told you. I go to prepare a place for you. And if I go and prepare a place for you, I will come again, and receive you unto myself; that where I am, there ye may be also (John 14:1-3).

"I will come again, and receive you unto myself." With these words of comfort for the disciples, the Lord Jesus Christ set His face to go to Calvary. Shocked beyond measure at the announcement of His death, these disciples were cheered with the "blessed hope" that He who was going away was coming again to receive them unto Himself, that they might be with Him. After the Resurrection of the Lord, as they stood upon Mount Olivet with Him, He was suddenly taken away from them into heaven, in fulfillment of His words in John 14 that He was going away. But scarcely had He been taken from their sight when He sent word back to them from heaven, with the same comforting assurance that He was coming back again. Luke gives us the first words which the ascended Lord sent back from glory. They are found in Acts 1:11:

> Ye men of Galilee, why stand ye gazing up into heaven? this same Jesus, which is taken up from you into heaven, shall so come in like manner as ye have seen him go into heaven.

The last promise of the Word of God before the canon of Scripture was closed is also concerning that blessed hope of the return of the One who went away, for we read in Revelation 22:20:

> He which testifieth these things saith, Surely I come quickly. Amen.

It is this "blessed hope" of the return of the Lord Jesus which has been the strength of God's people in every age, their comfort in affliction, their hope in trouble and their strength in battle. It was this hope that set on fire the early apostles as they bore the blessed news far and near and were faithful unto death. It was this hope of the imminent return of their Lord that kept their loins girded, their lamps burning and their eyes watching, lest coming upon them suddenly, He should find them sleeping.

CHRIST IS COMING SOON

Nineteen hundred years have passed since the last of these promises was given, and we today are just that many years nearer the time of which our Lord spoke. As the deepening shadows of the coming night of this world's judgment spread about us and we hear the thunder of the coming predicted storm, Christians are looking up, even as they have done since the promise was first given them — looking up in the same assurance of faith that He who said He would come will come, and will not tarry. We Christians have this advantage over the early Christians: we are nearer that event now than we have ever been by almost two millenniums. Add to this the fact that *all* the signs given in the Bible as heralding the coming of the Lord are being fulfilled before our very eyes. The wars and rumors of wars, false messiahs and false prophets, pestilences, famines, earthquakes, increasing anti-Semitism, the sea and waves roaring, apostasy, moral wickedness, political corruption and all the other indications are here simultaneously for the first time in history, and Jesus said in Luke 21:28:

> When these things begin to come to pass, then look up, and lift up your heads; for your redemption draweth nigh.

THE RAPTURE

The next prophetic event in the program of God is the catching away of all true believers before the final world crash of this dispensation. This catching away of the Church, preceded momentarily by the resurrection of all the righteous dead, is generally called *The Rapture*. The word "rapture" itself does not occur in the Bible, but we use it to express an event which is clearly and repeatedly taught. The fact that the word does not occur does not alter the fact. The word "Trinity" does not occur in the Scriptures either, or the expression "supernatural conception" or "virgin birth," but these terms express rather that which is taught in the Bible. "Rapture" is the word which expresses that event when Christ shall come again according to His promise to take away His Church in preparation for His reign with her on earth.

The word "rapture" comes from the Latin word *rapio*, which means "to snatch away suddenly." The English word "rapture" as applied to the Lord's return means "to carry away to sublime happiness." It is called in Titus "that blessed hope." In I Thessalonians 4:16, 17 we read:

> For the Lord himself shall descend from heaven with a shout, with the voice of the archangel, and with the trump of God: and the dead in Christ shall rise first: then we which are alive and remain shall be caught up together with them in the clouds, to meet the Lord in the air.

In I Corinthians 15:51, 52 we read of the suddenness of the event:

> We shall not all sleep, but we shall all be changed, in a moment, in the twinkling of an eye, at the last trump: for the trumpet shall sound, and the dead shall be raised incorruptible, and we shall be changed.

THE RAPTURE AND THE REVELATION

Most of the misunderstanding among Christians concerning the Rapture results from failure to distinguish between the Rapture and the Revelation of Christ at His second coming. Two phases of the second coming are sharply differentiated in Scripture so that it seems unreasonable that any who study the Bible should be confused. The Rapture is a joyous event, always associated with comfort and encouragement for God's people. The Revelation is a terrible event, when the Lord descends from heaven with flaming fire to take vengeance upon the

ungodly and destroy the wicked. Confusion of these two
or failure to distinguish both in time and character robs
one of the blessed hope.

Three words are used in connection with the second
coming of Christ. These three words are: *Parousia,
Apokalypsis* and *Epiphenia.* The first two are most com-
monly used when speaking of the Lord's return. The
Parousia refers generally to a period of time ushered in
by the return of the Lord for His Church — a time followed by the Tribulation period. This Tribulation period
on the earth will last for seven years and then at the close
of that period the Lord Jesus Christ will come in the
Apokalypsis. In the Parousia He will come only part of
the way from heaven to earth. He will come in the air,
and shout for His Church, and then she will be transported
by the Holy Spirit into the air, to meet the Lord there,
where He will keep her safely until He comes back with
her in the Revelation. The word *Parousia* literally means
"presence." At His descent in the air He will come to take
us into His presence. The word *Apokalypsis* means "unveiling," or as the Bible translates it, the "Revelation of
Jesus Christ."

THE PAROUSIA

The two events — the coming of Christ for His Church
before the Tribulation and His coming with the Church
after the Tribulation — are entirely different in character.
The Rapture is distinguished by four characteristics:
1. It is selective in character.
2. It is secret.
3. It is sudden, like the twinkling of an eye.
4. It is satisfying in full.

Only a select number will share in this first phase of the
coming of the Lord, and rise to meet Him in the air. Only
those who have been redeemed and washed in the blood of
the Lamb will hear that shout and rise to meet Him in
the air. In every passage where the event is mentioned it

is clearly indicated that none but the saved will share in this glorious, blessed event.

> The dead in Christ shall rise first.
> Christ the firstfruits; afterward they that are Christ's at his coming.

By His "secret" coming we mean that when the Lord comes for His Church only those who are waiting for Him will be caught up and all the others will not know what has happened until after the event has occurred. They may know that something has happened, but what it is they will not know. When the Lord spoke to Paul on the way to Damascus, the men which were with Him saw the light and were afraid, but they heard not the voice of Him that spoke to Paul. When the world awakes after the Rapture and finds every Christian gone, there will be great concern until the devil presents his lie in explanation of the sudden mysterious disappearance of those who have been raptured.

> Behold, I come as a thief. Blessed is he that watcheth, and keepeth his garments, lest he walk naked, and they see his shame. (Rev. 16:15).
> For yourselves know perfectly that the day of the Lord so cometh as a thief in the night. For when they shall say, Peace and safety; then sudden destruction cometh upon them, as travail upon a woman with child; and they shall not escape. But ye, brethren, are not in darkness, that that day should overtake you as a thief. Ye are all the children of light, and the children of the day: we are not of the night, nor of darkness (I Thess. 5:2-5).

HIS COMING WILL BE SUDDEN

The entire event will take place in a moment. So rapidly will Christians disappear that none of the unsaved will be able to see their departure. They will be looking at one another and suddenly while an unsaved husband is looking at his wife, she will be gone. A mother nursing her baby at her breast will suddenly feel her arms empty (unless she is saved and goes, too). She will be left holding only a handful of baby clothes. A crowd of people riding in a bus will suddenly feel the bus swerve and head for the ditch. They will notice that the driver has suddenly vanished into thin air without having opened a door or a window. Other passengers, too, will disappear, leaving only their clothes as evidence of their recent presence. Every word used in Scripture indicates the suddenness of the change. Paul says in I Corinthians 15 that it will be in the "twinkling of an eye" — not the winking but the "twinkling" of an eye. The same word used by Paul in I Thessalonians 4, translated "caught up," is also used of Philip in Acts 8:39, where we read:

> The Spirit of the Lord caught away Philip, that the eunuch saw him no more.

The same word is used again in II Corinthians 12:2-4 where Paul tells us that he was *"caught up into paradise."*

This event will be the consummation of all our hopes and longings. Instantly every believer will receive a new, glorified, sinless, painless, deathless body. He will be suddenly reunited with all his saved loved ones who have gone before, to dwell in fellowship with them forever. Best of all, then, we shall see Him, the Lord of Glory, who died for us on Calvary's Cross and intercedes for us now to keep us until that day. We shall see Him and be like Him, "for we shall see him as he is." How our hearts burn within us as we anticipate that glad day! One of these days, as surely as He came the first time, He is coming again. Were it not for this hope and the absolute faith in His promise, "I will come again," every incentive for going on would be taken away. Then, indeed, of all men, we would be "most miserable." But He is coming! Hallelujah!

We shall see Him, the King in His beauty. I have often tried to imagine that first thrill when, as we rise with wingless flight through the air to meet Him, we catch the first glimpse of His wonderful face and behold the Lord. All our troubles will be over. All the little sacrifices we have made for Him will then seem trivial and puny. David knew this and expressed it wonderfully in the Seventeenth Psalm. He had been observing that the wicked seem to prosper here on the earth, and he had had to suffer for Christ's sake. Then he cries:

> Deliver my soul from the wicked, which is thy sword: from men which are thy hand, O Lord, from men of the world, which have their portion in this life, and whose belly thou fillest with thy hid treasure: they are full of children, and leave the rest of their substance to their babes (Ps. 17:13, 14).

Then, lifting his eyes from the injustices of this earth, he declares in the next verse:

> As for me, I will behold thy face in righteousness: I shall be satisfied, when I awake, with thy likeness.
> Beloved, now are we the sons of God, and it doth not yet appear what we shall be: but we know that, when he shall appear, we shall be like him; for we shall see him as he is. And every man that hath this hope in him purifieth himself, even as he is pure (I John 3:2, 3).

II. THE PRE-TRIBULATION RAPTURE

> Watch ye therefore, and pray always, that ye may be accounted worthy to escape all these things that shall come to pass, and to stand before the Son of man (Luke 21:36).

One of the burning questions of the day and one which is arousing unusual interest is: Will the Church go through the Tribulation? Strange as it may seem, although Scripture shows that the very essence of the blessed hope is the hope of escaping the Tribulation, there are thousands of sincere and well-meaning Christians who have been misled into believing that the Church, the bride of Christ, will have to go through that awful day. Such are the trickeries of the enemy. The more important a doctrine is, the more Satan seeks to confuse God's people. It is easy to understand why he hates the truth of the imminent return of the Lord Jesus, for there is nothing in the world that will cause men to live watchfully and carefully as much as the expectation of His "any moment" return. This confusion among Christians has made it difficult to interest the unsaved in salvation, since they look at these differences and confusion among Christians and do not believe that salvation is real.

There are many schools of thought in regard to the time of the Rapture and who will be in it. There is the postmillennial teaching which sets the Rapture at the end of the world after the Millennium. Among the Premillennialists there are those who have divergent views also. Below are a few of the interpretations:

1. Pre-Tribulation Rapture of the entire Church.
2. Post-Tribulation Rapture of the entire Church.
3. Mid-Tribulation Rapturists.
4. Partial Rapturists who teach that only those who attain a certain degree of holiness will be taken up at the coming of Christ and the rest will have to endure the fires of the judgment of the Tribulation.

With all these various views and able teachers to champion them, it is no wonder that confusion has resulted. We should turn away from each and every one of man's views and limit ourselves to the Word of the Lord. "To the law and to the testimony: if they speak not according to this word, it is because there is no light in them."

TRIBULATION FOR ISRAEL

First of all, notice that in every passage of the Word where the Tribulation is mentioned it is with regard to Israel. The Church is never associated with or in it, but every reference to it fixes it as a time of judgment for Israel and the nations. In Jeremiah 30:7 it is called the "time of Jacob's trouble," and the following verses show that they will go through this day into millennial blessings. Daniel 12:1 states, in speaking of this day, "Thy people shall be delivered." "Thy People" were Daniel's people, Israel. Where Jesus speaks of that day it is always with reference to Israel, and His warnings are concerning Sabbath days' journeys and fleeing from Judea. The entire setting of every Tribulation passage is

Israelitish. There is no reference to the Church's being in it.

THE MAN OF SIN AND TRIBULATION

In the Second Epistle of Paul to the Thessalonian church, in the second chapter, we have a proof which, apart from any of the other Scriptural evidences, places the Rapture of the Church *before* the Day of the Lord. The Christians in Thessalonica had been greatly disturbed by a false report, forged in Paul's handwriting, that the Rapture had already passed and they had been left behind. This naturally alarmed them for they had been taught that before the Day of the Lord the Church would be taken away. They were expecting to escape the terrors of the Tribulation and the reason for their alarm was this very report that they had been left behind to go through the Tribulation. This is evident from the following verse:

> Now we beseech you, brethren, by the coming of our Lord Jesus Christ, and by our gathering together unto him, that ye be not soon shaken in mind, or be troubled, neither by spirit, nor by word, nor by letter from us, as that the day of the Lord were already here (II Thess. 2:1-2, literal translation).

These Christians were disturbed by a false report that the Day of the Lord (the Tribulation) was already present. If Paul had taught, as some do today, that the Church must pass through the Tribulation, then certainly they would have expected it and would not have been so disturbed. The very fact that these Christians were so troubled by the false report proves in itself that these Thessalonian Christians taught by Paul expected the Church to be taken out before the Day of the Lord.

PAUL'S ANSWER

When Paul hears of this confusion he immediately writes the letter to clarify the matter. He gives it to them so clearly that we wonder how Christians nineteen hundred years after can still be troubled about this matter:

> Let no man deceive you by any means [note well the warning against deception in regard to this truth]: for that day shall not come, except there come a falling away first, and that man of sin be revealed, the son of perdition (II Thess. 2:3).

This, then, is perfectly clear: that day cannot come until two things happen. First a "falling away" (the apostasy of the last days) followed by the revelation of the Man of Sin. The coming of the Antichrist will usher in and precede the Tribulation. Notice also verses 6 to 8:

> And now ye know what withholdeth that he [the Antichrist] might be revealed in his time. For the mystery of iniquity doth already work: only he who now letteth [hindreth] will let, until he be taken out of the way. And then shall that Wicked [lawless one] be revealed, whom the Lord shall consume with the spirit of his mouth, and shall destroy with the brightness of His coming (II Thess. 2:6-8).

The Holy Spirit who has dwelt in the body of Christ, the Church, since Pentecost, and will, according to Christ, abide with us during this age, is here called the Restrainer, the One who holds back the revelation of the Man of Sin. The Antichrist cannot be revealed until the indwelling Spirit in the Church is taken out of the way. Immediately after the Spirit takes the Church away, then shall that lawless one be revealed, only to be destroyed when the Lord Jesus comes back to the earth with His bride. Put these two facts together. First the Day of the Lord will not come till the Man of Sin is revealed. But the Man of Sin cannot be revealed until He who now restrains is taken out of the way. So you see, this second fact coupled with the first makes it absolutely impossible for the Day of the Lord to come until after the Church has been taken away. Surely Scripture can be no plainer.

THE TESTIMONY OF TYPE

In speaking of His second coming the Lord Jesus Christ referred to two incidents in history as pictures of the days that would precede His coming again. The one was the Flood of Noah and the other was the destruction of the cities of the plain, Sodom and Gomorrah. In each case we have a type of the Rapture as preceding the coming of judgment. In the case of the Flood, Enoch who walked with God was taken out before the storm broke. In the case of the destruction of Sodom, Lot and his two daughters were led out by the angels before the fire fell. Surely it was not accidental that Jesus should have chosen just these two incidents from history to teach the truth of His coming again. Enoch is the type of the spiritual man raptured before the Tribulation, of which the Flood was an evident type. Lot and his daughters were the worldly believers, for the Scriptures tell us that Lot was a righteous man, vexed with the filthiness of Sodom, yet they were taken to safety before the fire came down from heaven. There will be two classes of people at the judgment seat of Christ immediately after the Rapture, and these two classes are represented by Enoch and Lot — those who will have "confidence" at His appearing and those who will be "ashamed." Some will receive a reward and others will suffer loss. Both classes will be there, however, even though some shall receive rewards and have an "abundant entrance," whereas others "shall be saved; yet so as by fire."

THE RAPTURE IN REVELATION

Add to all this evidence in type the teaching of the very structure of the book of Revelation. In chapters 2 and 3 of Revelation we have a picture of the history of the Church during the absence of our Lord. This runs its course from Pentecost to His coming for the Church, and is described by the picture of the seven literal churches of Asia Minor beginning with Ephesus and ending with Laodicea. In these two chapters the Church is mentioned *fourteen times*. Notice Revelation 4:1-2:

> After this I looked, and, behold, a door was opened in heaven: and the first voice which I heard was as it were of a trumpet talking with me; which said, Come up hither, and I will shew thee things which must be hereafter. And immediately I was in the spirit: and, behold, a throne was set in heaven, and one sat on the throne.

What follows in Revelation 6 to 19 is conceded by all to be the most vivid description in the Bible of the Tribulation period. Before the Tribulation was described, however, John was called into heaven and from there beheld the things which were to follow. The Church was gone. She never again was seen on the earth, according to the book of Revelation. Before this she was mentioned no less than fourteen times in chapters 2 and 3 as being on earth. After John was caught away, the Church disappeared from the earth, and during all the time that follows we see Israel and the nations but not the bride. She is with her Lord. Chapter 19 tells of her return with her Lord to reign with Him on the earth.

DIRECT SCRIPTURE

We have been dealing with a number of incidents in type and symbol which teach the pre-Tribulation Rapture of the Church. The Holy Spirit is so jealous of this important truth that He has given us, in addition, a great many direct passages which permit of no twisting and misinterpretation. We shall notice a few.

> Ye turned to God from idols to serve the living and true God; and to wait for his Son from heaven, whom he raised from the dead . . . which delivered us from the wrath to come (I Thess. 1:9-10).

In chapter 5 of this same epistle Paul speaks of the coming of the Lord as a thief in the night and warns the Christians to be watchful and waiting. He gives this as the motive: "For God hath not appointed us to wrath, but to obtain salvation by our Lord Jesus Christ." This salvation is a future salvation and refers to escaping the "wrath of God" when He comes to judge the earth.

There is one passage which fell from the lips of the Lord Jesus Himself which dispels all doubts as to whether the Church shall see even a part of that awful day of trouble. It is found in the same chapter which describes so vividly that day of Jacob's trouble (see Luke

21). In this chapter the disciples asked the Lord concerning the time and the signs preceding the destruction of Jerusalem and the Lord's return. He tells them of the wars and rumors of wars and of the awful turmoil on the earth just before that day. Then He describes in detail the conditions which will prevail on the earth:

> And when ye shall see Jerusalem compassed with armies, then know that the desolation thereof is nigh. Then let them which are in Judaea flee to the mountains; and let them which are in the midst of it depart out; and let not them that are in the countries enter thereinto. For these be the days of vengeance, that all things which are written may be fulfilled. But woe unto them that are with child, and to them that give suck, in those days! for there shall be great distress in the land, and wrath upon this people (Luke 21:20-23).
>
> And take heed to yourselves, lest at any time your hearts be overcharged with surfeiting, and drunkenness, and cares of this life, and so that day come upon you unawares. For as a snare shall it come on all them that dwell on the face of the whole earth (Luke 21:34-35).

This is but a part of the description of that awful day. It is elaborated upon in Matthew, Mark and the entire book of Revelation. After having warned the apostles, the Lord Jesus adds a most significant verse in Luke 21:36:

> Watch ye therefore, and pray always, that ye may be accounted worthy to escape all these things that shall come to pass, and to stand before the Son of man.

There will then be a watching and praying company who will escape all these things which are coming to pass. That, beloved, is the blessed hope.

THAT BLESSED HOPE

The believer has a blessed hope. How the devil would like to take that away from us in these dark days, and how he has succeeded in deluding many Christians into looking for the Tribulation instead of the coming of the Lord! If the Church must pass through the Tribulation, then the Church is looking for the Antichrist instead of the Christ, for the Antichrist will reign during the Tribulation. Where, then, is the blessed hope? What, then, is this

blessed hope? It is this: we are expecting and looking
for the Lord Jesus Christ to come *before* the Antichrist
is revealed.

Friend, what is your blessed hope? One of these days
the Lord is coming and then everything will depend upon
what you do with Him *now*.

> Because thou hast kept the word of my patience, I also
> will keep thee from the hour of temptation, which shall come
> upon all the world, to try them that dwell upon the earth
> (Rev. 3:10).

III. THE RESURRECTION BODY

"The wages of sin is death." Thus does the Bible sum
up the awful result of man's transgression. This death is
more than spiritual death; it includes also physical death.
The moment that Adam sinned he died spiritually, he
broke with his God and became "dead in trespasses and
sins." But the moment he sinned he also died physically.
Although he lived some 950 years after he fell, the sentence of physical death passed upon him immediately, and
he began to die, and it was only a matter of time until he
returned to the earth from which he was taken. Thus
death passed upon all men for that all have sinned. From
that time on, with only two exceptions, it has been the lot
of all Adam's children to come into the world to die.
From the day of birth the processes of decay are working
in our bodies, and life here on earth is but a living death.

But "as in Adam all die, even so in Christ shall all be
made alive." The last Adam restores that which the first
Adam lost. The first Adam brought death; the last Adam
brings life. As the death by sin was delayed so far as the
physical body was concerned, so the redemption of the
body is delayed until the coming of Christ. The moment
Adam sinned he died spiritually but his physical death
came hundreds of years later. In the very same way, when
the last Adam paid the price for sin on the Cross He made
available immediately spiritual life and ultimately, as
well, eternal physical life. The moment one believes on

the Lord Jesus Christ he becomes spiritually alive, but the final redemption of the body is postponed until the Lord Jesus comes again. We who are saved still have our mortal bodies, and if the Lord tarries, these bodies will be laid in the grave. But at the coming of the Lord for His Church these bodies also shall be changed and made like unto the glorious body of our Lord Jesus Christ.

THE DEAD RAISED

This resurrection of the bodies of believers is the first event which will follow the shout of the Lord from the air when He comes to receive His Church. The dead in Christ shall rise first and then we who are alive and remain until His coming shall be suddenly changed in the twinkling of an eye. In the first letter of Paul to the Corinthians we find that Paul, under inspiration, devotes one entire chapter to this great event, and gives a detailed description of these resurrection bodies, which all believers dead and alive will receive at that time. This resurrection body must not be confused with the "house which is from heaven." According to II Corinthians 5 there are bodies which the saints put on when they die and in which they dwell "until" the coming of the Lord, when they, too, receive their eternal glorious resurrection bodies.

> For we know that if our earthly house of this tabernacle were dissolved, we have a building of God, an house not made with hands, eternal in the heavens. For in this we groan, earnestly desiring to be clothed upon with our house which is from heaven: if so be that being clothed we shall not be found naked. For we that are in this tabernacle do groan, being burdened: not for that we would be unclothed, but clothed upon, that mortality might be swallowed up of life (II Cor. 5:1-4).

Surely there seems to be a reference here to a "clothing upon" which takes place immediately at the dissolution of this earthly tabernacle. Bodies are given to those who fall asleep in Christ. In these they dwell while waiting for the coming again of Christ to give to all their glorious resurrection bodies. Our loved ones gone before are not naked in heaven. They are not disembodied spirits, but clothed with vestments provided by the Lord. They are visible. John saw the souls of those who were beheaded for the cause of Christ. Disembodied spirits are not visible. When Moses and Elijah appeared on the Mount of Transfiguration, they were visible and had bodies. Theirs could not have been the same bodies that they had here on earth, for those were sinful bodies and therefore could not be admitted to heaven. God is able to clothe spirits. The appearance of angels in the Old and New Testaments in visible forms indicates that God can clothe spirits in bodies for temporary service and then lay them aside again when the work is done. So it seems that in the interval between the death of the saints and their resurrection at Christ's coming they have a "house not made with hands" that they might not appear "naked," but be clothed upon. Just what this "clothing" is the Bible does not say, but, while we would not dogmatize too strongly here, this does indicate some provision for our spirits in heaven after death until we receive our new bodies at His coming.

THE NEW BODIES

Whether we agree as to the above or not, one thing all Christians do believe is that when Jesus comes all the saints' bodies shall arise. Not one will be overlooked. Those who perished in the sea, they that were burned to ashes, they that were devoured by wild beasts or died in other ways — all shall be raised. The objection is often raised that this cannot be, since the bodies of those who died hundreds or thousands of years ago have disintegrated and have been transformed into other bodies and, therefore, the elements which composed one body a thousand years ago may be part of other bodies today. Let me illustrate. Let us imagine a man who lived a thousand years ago. His body consisted of 150 pounds of elements such as oxygen, hydrogen, sodium, potassium and a number of others. When his body died it was placed in the ground and deteriorated. A tree grew over the grave and its roots absorbed the various elements which were once the body of this man. They became part of the tree. The tree bore fruit. A cow ate the fruit containing many of the elements which were part of the body of that man. They became part of the cow. The cow was butchered, and the meat was eaten by other men so that these men were literally eating the other man who had died, for the same elements which composed his body became part of their bodies. Then these men died and their bodies were buried and grass grew over their graves and ultimately their bodies were absorbed by the roots of plants, and the plants were eaten again by animals. We find that the elements which composed the body of the first man who died became part of a thousand men and women. You can see how the bodies of the dead cannot be brought back atom by atom as they were originally. Certain individual atoms may belong to a thousand different bodies, and since no body can occupy two places at once, this makes it impossible for the actual body which was buried to arise with its original component atoms and molecules.

This argument has been advanced by skeptics to deny the literal resurrection. The Bible, however, anticipated this objection, and has answered it in I Corinthians 15:

> But some man will say, How are the dead raised up? and with what body do they come? Thou fool, that which thou sowest is not quickened, except it die: and that which thou sowest, thou sowest not that body that shall be, but bare grain, it may chance of wheat, or of some other grain: but God giveth it a body as it hath pleased him, and to every seed his own body. All flesh is not the same flesh: but there is one kind of flesh of men, another flesh of beasts, another of fishes, and another of birds. There are also celestial bodies, and bodies terrestrial: but the glory of the celestial is one, and the glory of the terrestrial is another. There is one glory of the sun, and another glory of the moon, and another glory of the stars: for one star differeth from another star in glory. So also is the resurrection of the dead (I Cor. 15:35-42).

This passage contains the answer to our question. Paul says there is a flesh of men, of beasts, of birds and of fish. They differ in form but are composed of the same elements, and the elements in one may become the elements in another, as when we eat fish or birds or fish and birds eat men. It is not the particular atoms which count, but the individual. So also is the resurrection of the dead. The same elements which were laid in the grave will not necessarily be brought together, but the individual will be the same. It is a scientific fact that the component elements of our bodies are constantly interchanging. We are constantly taking in new elements in food, drink and air and throwing off others as waste to be absorbed by other organisms. It is said that we receive through this interchange of elements a new body every seven years. Not one atom now in your body will be there seven years from now. Yet this fact of an entire change of atoms does not change *you* as an individual. These elements are not *you*, but the soul that dwells in them. Your body today still has the same physical characteristics it possessed seven years ago, though it is composed of entirely new atoms.

THE SEED OF WHEAT

Paul further illustrates this when he refers to the planting of a grain of wheat. He says, "And that which thou sowest, thou sowest not that body that shall be, but bare grain." Assume that you sow a grain of wheat which bears a hundred other kernels. These kernels are not a multiplication of the same elements which were sown but are composed of different elements taken up from the soil and from the air. Now we have a new kernel composed of different individual atoms of matter, but it is still a kernel of wheat. It bears all the characteristics of the kernel which was sown. It is not the same kernel, and yet it is identically like the one which was sown. It is the same in color, texture and consistency, and, under normal conditions, even the same in size and appearance. It is a kernel of wheat like the one that died and was buried. Now it is raised. It is a new kernel containing some of the elements and all of the characteristics of the original. So also is the resurrection of the dead. The resurrection body is the same body, and yet it is different.

> It is sown in corruption; it is raised in incorruption: it is sown in dishonour; it is raised in glory: it is sown in weakness; it is raised in power: it is sown a natural body; it is raised a spiritual body. There is a natural body, and there is a spiritual body (I Cor. 15:42-44).

There is a tremendous difference between that which is sown and that which is raised, and yet the identity and the nature are not lost. The wheat is still wheat which resembles the seed that was sown in every way. It is different; yet it is the same. So also is the resurrection of the dead. This alone should answer the question which is so frequently asked —

WILL WE RECOGNIZE ONE ANOTHER IN HEAVEN?

Yes, indeed, you will recognize your loved ones in heaven. They will have new bodies which will resemble the bodies they had here on earth. All the characteristics will be there just as surely as the new grain of wheat resembles the old kernel that was sown. Their bodies will be without the blemishes, weaknesses and disabilities they now have. Yes, you will recognize that blind child of yours in heaven; but she will not be blind. That paralyzed boy who lies there as you read this message will be there, and you will know him as your darling son; but he will not be paralyzed. Yes, we shall know one another up there and enjoy one another in a closer, sweeter fellowship than that of father and son, mother and daughter or husband and wife.

THE CATERPILLAR AND THE BUTTERFLY

Although our bodies will resemble the bodies we have now, they will be so much more glorious than these that it is difficult to describe. Paul tries it by using the contrasting terms, corruption and incorruption, dishonor and glory, weakness and power, natural and spiritual. In Philippians 3:20-21 we read:

> For our conversation is in heaven; from whence also we look for the Saviour, the Lord Jesus Christ: who shall change our vile body, that it may be fashioned like unto his glorious body.

Literally Paul says, "Who shall change these bodies of our humiliation and *metamorphose* them into the likeness of the body of his glory." He will *metamorphose* our bodies. The word is from two Greek words meaning "to change the fashion of." We speak of the change of a caterpillar into a butterfly as a "metamorphosis." Picture an ugly, slimy, repulsive caterpillar. We shrink from it as it wriggles and squirms threateningly. After a while, however, it is put into a tomb which it spins for itself. It apparently disintegrates, and if you were to open the cocoon in the winter you would find only a chrysalis full of repulsive, apparently dead, formless, viscous fluid. But the warm sun of the spring beats upon the tomb of the caterpillar, and one day there comes forth not an ugly caterpillar but a beautiful — yes, superlatively beautiful — butterfly, gracefully drying its wings as they unfold in the light and sparkle with a breath-taking irridescent beauty. Yes, it is the same caterpillar that was entombed the previous autumn and yet it is different. If we are familiar with insects we recognize that butterfly as being the same as the caterpillar. We identify them easily. So also shall be the resurrection of the dead. Yes, we shall know our loved ones, but, oh, how different they will be! Everything will be different and yet we will see the same dear loved ones who said good-bye as we wept at their bedsides.

How our hearts long for that day when the "Lord himself shall descend from heaven with a shout, with the voice of the archangel, and with the trump of God: and the dead in Christ shall rise first: then we which are alive and remain shall be caught up together with them in the clouds, to meet the Lord in the air." We, too, can shout:

O death, where is thy sting? O grave, where is thy victory?

IV. RECOGNITION IN HEAVEN

For now we see through a glass, darkly; but then face to face; now I know in part; but then shall I know even as also I am known (I Cor. 13:12).

When the Lord Jesus comes to call His Church and we are changed in a moment, in the twinkling of an eye, the thrills will come so thick and fast that we will need resurrection and glorified bodies to endure the excitement of that glad meeting. These poor bodies would utterly collapse at the glory of that glad hour. We shall be like Him and see Him as He is, and then we shall meet our loved ones and be forever with them and with the Lord. There is a great deal more evidence in the Word for absolute recognition in heaven than the figure of the wheat which we gave in our previous message. The Bible leaves no doubt about the matter.

MOSES AND ELIJAH

On the Mount of Transfiguration the three disciples of the Lord not only saw the Lord Jesus glorified but with Him were two men whom they *recognized* as Moses and Elijah. These disciples had never met these two men, and yet they recognized them immediately. Whether it was by their appearance is of no importance. The point is: they *knew* them when they *saw* them. Elijah had been gone for seven hundred years but they recognized him. Moses had been dead for almost two thousand years and then had been raised from the dead, but the disciples recognized him also.

The Lord Jesus Himself tells us that there will be recognition after death. In Luke we have the story of the rich man and Lazarus. The rich man died and went to hades, and the poor man went to the bosom of Abraham. Abraham and Lazarus were not only visible to the rich man in torment, but he recognized both of them. He recognized Lazarus as the one who had lain at his gate begging, and he recognized Abraham from the descriptions of the patriarch which he must have heard. If the damned in the pit recognize each other after death, will the Lord grant to us less than He does to the lost?

Our resurrection bodies will be like His body (the Lord's) and so when we study what Scripture has to say about His body we will know the nature of ours. First of all, our Lord's Resurrection body was like His earthly body in appearance. It carried the identification marks whereby the disciples might know that it was He. If you object and say that they did not recognize Him when they first met Him, we answer with the remark that the Scripture definitely states that "their eyes were holden" that they should not recognize Him. But when "their eyes were opened" they saw immediately who He was. He carried the marks of the nails in His hands and feet and the scar of the spear in His side. The scars were healed, though only three days before those hands, feet and side had been pierced. In His new body He carried the marks, but they were healed. Yes, and in our new bodies, too, every wound will be healed and every tear will be dried.

THE PREPARATION OF THE BRIDE

The meeting in the air and the reunion with our loved ones and Him will be only the beginning of our joy. We will be caught up into the clouds with Him, and then while He purifies the earth in the Tribulation in preparation for His glorious reign, the Church will be in the air, being made ready for the wedding of the Lamb and the royal honeymoon. While the Lord judges the nations on earth, He will judge His people in heaven at the judgment seat of Christ. This judgment is not connected with our salvation, for that was settled when we believed, but it has to do with the matter of rewards, the places we shall be given at the wedding supper, the crowns we shall wear and the position we shall hold for one thousand years in the millennial reign of Christ. On that judgment will depend whether we shall reign over ten cities or over five, or whether we shall be given a smaller and less honorable place in that kingdom. At the judgment seat of Christ the wrongs which you failed to right here will be made right. Some of you who have been too proud to humble yourselves here and confess your faults will have to do it there, before you are fit to go into the wedding feast of the Lamb.

The judgment seat of Christ which follows the Rapture will not be a pleasant experience for all. There will be suffering and rebukes there, cleansing and confessing and real sorrow as men and women lose their rewards and are saved "yet so as by fire." Some will be rewarded, and others will suffer loss as they see the hay, wood and stubble go up in smoke and the Lord tells them to take a lower place at His footstool. Many of you refuse to cleanse yourselves by the washing of the Word here, and will have to go through the fires of the judgment seat there. It is not going to be a pleasant experience.

THE WEDDING GARMENT

In olden times the bride made her own wedding dress. Today you can get it "already made" the day before you get married if you wish. But in days of old it was the pride of the bride that she had stitched her own wedding dress. The bride of the Lord Jesus Christ, too, will have a hand in making her own wedding dress. Of course, we know that every member of the bride is already clothed in the garments of the Lord's righteousness. The moment we believe on Him He imputed to us His righteousness and we were saved. There is also another righteousness which will be worn on that glad day. This righteousness is the garments we make while here below and they will consist of the "good works of faith" which we have laid up, adorned with the gold, silver and precious stones of our service that will abide in that day. Let no Christian think that because he is saved it makes no difference how he lives. There is a reckoning coming, and for those who think thus it will be a sad, sad reckoning. "Be not deceived; God is not mocked: for whatsoever a man soweth, that shall he also reap."

ACCORDING TO THEIR WORKS

For we must all appear before the judgment seat of Christ; that every one may receive the things done in his body, according to that he hath done, whether it be good or bad (II Cor. 5:10).

Salvation depends on grace and grace alone. By it God imputes to you His righteousness. There is another righteousness, however, which is *practical* and not *positional*. The first determines your salvation; the second determines your reward. God makes you ready to be saved, but you must make yourself ready to reign. You can either get ready here or wait until you must do it up there. I assure you that it will be more pleasant, satisfactory and profitable to do it *now*.

SANCTIFICATION AND CLEANSING

In Ephesians 5:26 we are told that Christ will sanctify and cleanse His Church by the washing of water by the Word. The two words used, "sanctify" and "cleanse," are not the same in the Greek. The word translated "sanctify" is *hagarizo* and means "to purify by washing." The word translated "cleanse" in this verse is *katharizo*, from which our English word "cathartic" comes. God has two ways of making us clean: by "sanctifying" by washing of water by the Word. If we refuse this method, then He will give us a "cathartic," but He will have us clean. How much better it is to take the gentler course now, than to wait until the judgment seat of Christ to be purged by fire!

THE WEDDING GOWN

In Revelation 19:7 we read:

Let us be glad and rejoice, and give honour to him: for the marriage of the Lamb is come, and his wife hath made herself ready.

Notice carefully that this is after the Tribulation and just before the coming of the Lord to set up the kingdom (Rev. 19:11). Revelation 4 tells of the Rapture of the Church, and the chapters following this to the nineteenth describe the seven years of tribulation during which time the bride is in the dressing room getting ready for the wedding. There are many alterations to be made, and the entire seven years are required to complete this task which should have been finished here below, before the Rapture. Finally the last button has been set over and the spots and stains have been washed, the hay, wood and stubble has been burned, and we read:

> The marriage of the Lamb is come, and his wife hath made herself ready.

Note what follows:

> And to her was granted that she should be arrayed in fine linen, clean and white: for the fine linen is the righteousness of saints.

The margin of my Bible translates this as "the *right-eousness* of the saints." The word is plural and means the "righteous acts" of the saints. She is adorned by her "good works" which remained after the testing at the judgment seat of Christ. Everything which was in the interest of self and of the flesh will have been burned out and only that which was done for the love of Christ will remain. That which remains of the precious stones will be worn as the garment for the wedding. O Christian, there needs to be a burning out in our lives, and if it is not done here it must be done up there.

> Only one life, 'twill soon be past;
> Only what's done for Christ will last.

THE WEDDING SUPPER

Next comes the wedding supper. All things are prepared, the table is set and the bride is ready and fit to take her place with her Lord at the table.

> And he saith unto me, Write, Blessed are they which are called unto the marriage supper of the Lamb. And he saith unto me, These are the true sayings of God (Rev. 19:9).

At this wedding supper we shall see the consummation of all our hopes and desires and all the hopes and desires of our blessed Lord. As in any well-ordered wedding, every group will be represented. God will be the Host at the wedding. The Father will be there to smile His benediction on the participants at the wedding. Also present will be the Son as the Groom who went through death to gain His precious bride. Next to Him will be the bride, who though unworthy in herself was made worthy by Him who gave His life for her. The guests will also be present. One cannot have a wedding without guests. These are called in the Scriptures the *friends* of the Bridegroom and consist of all the Old Testament saints who were raised at the first resurrection with the Church. They are not the bride, but they are the guests, the friends of the Bridegroom. In the Song of Solomon they are called the "daughters of Jerusalem." John the Baptist was one of the Old Testament saints who died before the Cross and he calls himself a *friend* of the Bridegroom.

GROUPED IN FAMILIES

There seems to be a suggestion in Scripture that we shall be grouped in families — in groups of fellowship resembling the groups in which we moved here below. The expressions in the Bible such as "he . . . was gathered unto his people" suggest that after death the saints went to their own family groups. Be that as it may, we shall *all* be there if we have been washed in the blood of the Lamb.

THE WAITERS

At the wedding there will also be waiters. The Scriptures tell us who they will be. We shall be served by the angels of God. Not only shall we judge angels, but they shall be our servants for we shall be wedded to the Lord of the house. In Hebrews 1:14 we read of the angels:

> Are they not all ministering servants, sent forth to minister for them who shall be heirs of salvation?

The supper will follow. What a feast it will be! Some of the things we shall eat are mentioned in the Bible. Jesus says in Revelation 2:7:

> To him that overcometh will I give to eat of the tree of life, which is in the midst of the paradise of God.

That fruit which was barred from Adam after he sinned "lest he eat of it and live forever" will be given us first so that we will never more be able to die. That tree is now in heaven and will be found in great groves on either side of the river in the New Jerusalem. That will be the first course. In Revelation 2:17 we read:

> To him that overcometh will I give to eat of the hidden manna.

The angels' food will be given to the saints. Moses placed a portion of the miraculous manna in a golden pot to be preserved forever. God knows where that pot of manna is, and will bring it out at that time. Jesus will increase it as He did the loaves and the fishes and give it to all of us. There will also be the water of life and the bread of life, for Christ is that living bread. There will be honey and the honeycomb, for David says God's Word is like honey, and we know that His Word will never perish but abide forever. What a feast! But best of all we will feast on Him. He said, "Except ye eat the flesh of the son of man, and drink his blood." Through all eternity our souls shall be satisfied and we cry out with rapturous anticipation, "How long, O Lord, how long?" Does not your heart burn as you think of this? Christians, are you ready? Are your garments clean? Soon He will come and we shall meet Him and be with Him forever.

> It may be at morn, when the day is awaking,
> When sunlight thro' darkness and shadow is breaking,
> That Jesus will come in the fullness of glory,
> To receive from the world "His own."
>
> It may be at midday, it may be at twilight,
> It may be, perchance, that the blackness of midnight
> Will burst into light in the blaze of His glory,
> When Jesus receives "His own."

Oh, joy! oh, delight! should we go without dying;
No sickness, no sadness, no dread, and no crying,
Caught up thro' the clouds with our Lord into glory
When Jesus receives "His own."
O Lord Jesus, how long, how long
Ere we shout the glad song, Christ returneth?
Hallelujah, hallelujah! Amen.

V. THE APOCALYPSE

The Revelation of the Lord Jesus Christ at His second coming *after* the Tribulation is in sharp contrast to His appearing for His Church at the beginning of the Tribulation. The first phase will be secret, sudden, selective, and satisfying, but His coming with His saints to judge the earth will be —

1. Public.
2. Paralyzing.
3. Punitive.

There are two classes of Scripture passages which speak of the coming again of Christ. These are very easy to recognize and differentiate if we bear in mind a few simple principles, some of which we have already suggested. The Rapture, or the secret coming, is seldom directly mentioned except in type in the Old Testament. Virtually all the references in the Old Testament deal with the glorious appearing at the close of the Tribulation and the commencement of the Millennium. In the New Testament, however, we find both aspects of the Lord's coming mentioned. The reason for this becomes immediately clear when we remember that the Rapture has to do with the Church only, whereas the Revelation has to do with Israel and the nations. In the Old Testament days there was no Church. That was a mystery not revealed until after the Day of Pentecost and then revealed by the Holy Spirit through Paul and the other apostles. The Old Testament saints and prophets knew nothing about the Church. She did not come into existence until after the rejection of the Lord at His first coming. It was this mystery —

> Which in other ages was not made known unto the sons of men, as it is now revealed unto his holy apostles and prophets by the Spirit; that the Gentiles should be fellow-heirs, and of the same body, and partakers of his promise in Christ by the gospel (Eph. 3:5-6).

Peter, in speaking of the Church as the body of Christ, tells us that even the prophets which spoke in the Old Testament did not understand their own utterances when they referred to that mystery age, and he says, speaking of this dispensation:

> Of which salvation the prophets have enquired and searched diligently, who prophesied of the grace that should come unto you: searching what, or what manner of time the Spirit of Christ which was in them did signify, when it testified beforehand the sufferings of Christ, and the glory that should follow (I Peter 1:10-11).

The Old Testament prophets saw two things — the Cross and the crown. They saw the suffering of Christ and the glory that should follow. These two things were clearly outlined. They did not see, however, the intervening time between the suffering and the glory. That was the Church Age, the age of the mystery of the body. This puzzled them greatly. They could see that Christ was to suffer and also to reign, but how these two could be they understood not. They failed to see the present age of the Holy Spirit. Everything connected with the future Church was a mystery to the Old Testament saints. When the Holy Spirit came on Pentecost He revealed this mystery of the Church, and we know now that in the eternal purpose of God, the kingdom of Israel was to be postponed at the Lord's first coming and to be resumed at His second coming. In the interval of Israel's rejection, the Holy Spirit was to call out the Church and after she is caught away, God will again begin to deal with His people Israel.

OLD TESTAMENT MYSTERY

The Church was born at Pentecost. There was no Church in the Old Testament. That was a kingdom age. Now you will see why the Rapture is never clearly spoken of in the Old Testament. The Rapture is for the Church and not for the kingdom. After Pentecost and the birth of the Church, the Holy Spirit began to reveal Church truth, the mystery of the Rapture and the mystery of Israel's setting aside. The prophecies of Israel abound with hundreds of references to the coming of the King, but they all look forward to the Revelation, not to the Rapture. We stated before that this Revelation, in sharp contrast to the secret, selective and satisfying aspects of the Rapture, would be public, paralyzing and punitive.

HIS COMING WILL BE PUBLIC

When the Lord Jesus Christ comes to the earth the second time every living creature on earth shall see Him. This is the universal testimony of Scripture. Israel shall see Him and shall recognize Him as the One who was slain on the Cross of Calvary as their Messiah and King.

> And I will pour upon the house of David, and upon the inhabitants of Jerusalem, the spirit of grace and of supplications: and they shall look upon me whom they have pierced, and they shall mourn for him, as one mourneth for his only son, and shall be in bitterness for him, as one that is in bitterness for his first born (Zech. 12:10).
> And one shall say unto him, What are these wounds in thine hands? Then he shall answer, Those with which I was wounded in the house of my friends (Zech. 13:6).

Not only will He be seen by repentant Israel but also by the nations, who then will be gathered to the north of Jerusalem for the great battle of Armageddon. Suddenly from the sky the Lord of Glory will appear in flaming fire to punish the inhabitants for their sin.

> Behold, he cometh with clouds; and every eye shall see him, and they also which pierced him: and all kindreds of the earth shall wail because of him (Rev. 1:7).

HIS COMING WILL BE PARALYZING

After the Church is taken out, the Holy Spirit is removed and all restraint is lifted from the earth, Satan will have a free hand. He will manifest His master stroke in the revelation of the world's superman — the Man of Sin called the Antichrist. This will be the devil's "short day."

He will assemble all the nations of the world in the greatest world war. Befriending Israel first, he will, after a brief period of three and a half years, turn suddenly upon them and seek to destroy them. All nations will be mobilized into four great armies, called in the Scriptures the Northern Army, the King of the South, the King of the East and the Western Empire of the restored old Roman Empire. These will vie for the prize of Palestine and will assemble in the world's most ideal battleground in the valley of Jehoshaphat, between the sheltering hills of Megiddo, situated in Palestine to the north of Jerusalem. The Bible is replete with vivid descriptions of this great coming battle at the eastern end of the Mediterranean. Note a few of them:

> Assemble yourselves, and come, all ye heathen, and gather yourselves together round about . . . Let the heathen be wakened, and come up to the valley of Jehoshaphat: for there will I sit to judge all the heathen round about . . . Multitudes, multitudes in the valley of decision: for the day of the Lord is near in the valley of decision (Joel 3:11, 12, 14).

> Behold, the day of the Lord cometh, and thy spoil shall be divided in the midst of thee. For I will gather all nations against Jerusalem to battle; and the city shall be taken, and the houses rifled, and the women ravished; and half of the city shall go forth into captivity, and the residue of the people shall not be cut off from the city. Then shall the Lord go forth, and fight against those nations, as when he fought in the day of battle (Zech. 14:1-3).

The result of this sudden coming of Christ will be the utter defeat of the enemies of Israel and the destruction of the armies of Satan. John, the writer of the Apocalypse, gives us the last blazing picture of this paralyzing time in Revelation 19:

> And I saw heaven opened, and behold a white horse; and he that sat upon him was called Faithful and True, and in righteousness he doth judge and make war (Rev. 19:11).

> And out of his mouth goeth a sharp sword, that with it he should smite the nations: and he shall rule them with a rod of iron: and he treadeth the wine press of the fierceness and wrath of Almighty God (Rev. 19:15).

> And the beast was taken, and with him the false prophet . . . These both were cast alive into a lake of fire . . . And

the remnant were slain with the sword of him that sat upon
the horse, which sword proceedeth out of his mouth: and
all the fowls were filled with their flesh (Rev. 19:20, 21).

After the enemy has been defeated and after a brief
period in which He will remove the wreckage of the war,
Jesus Christ will sit to judge the earth for one thousand
blessed years.

HIS COMING WILL BE PUNITIVE

The second coming will not only be public and paralyzing; it will be punitive. It will be in perfect justice and
in righteousness. God will reward the atrocities of the
ages on the basis of what the nations have done to God's
people. Those nations which have befriended the people
of God in their dispersion and affliction will receive the
kingdom blessing. Those who have oppressed them will
be utterly destroyed.

We have gone to great lengths to indicate the difference in character and time of the two phases of the Lord's
second coming. There is first His coming for His Church
— a secret, sudden, satisfying experience. Then, after
God has permitted Satan to rally the armies of the earth
and prove the utter incorrigibility of the human heart, He
will return in the stunning, paralyzing glory of His judgment. Would that the nations today knew that there is a
reckoning coming! Already the scene of action is shift-
ing to the very geographical center of the earth where
the greatest battle of all ages is to be fought. The armies
of the world are massing themselves in the greatest
mobilization of history. The steady gravitation of these
armies has been to the very spot where the last battle is
to be fought. It will be a battle which will make all other
previous conflicts seem like mere child's play.

WHO IS YOUR CAPTAIN?

In that great battle there will be two great leaders:
Christ and the Antichrist; God and the devil. You, my
friend, will belong either to the Lord's army or the devil's

army. You will either be of that company who will be caught away to meet the Lord in the Rapture or of those who will be left behind to join the armies of Satan and be doomed to defeat and everlasting disgrace. The outcome is already determined. The Bible states clearly that Jesus Christ will be the victor. I have by the grace of God volunteered in His army and can say, "I am on the Lord's side." There is no conscription in either army. What will your answer be? As this message comes to you, the devil is preparing his followers for the great slaughter, and the Lord Jesus is ready to call His ambassadors home for a brief period of instruction and preparation, to return with them to take the kingdom of the world as the kingdoms of our Lord and of His Christ.

Friend, are you ready for that day? Common sense teaches that we are in this world only for a little while, and then comes a long, long eternity. Your preparation now will determine your destiny in that great eternity. Christ is calling for volunteers. Will you be one of those who are "wise"? Make your choice of leaders *now.*

CHAPTER THREE

When Jesus Comes

I

The wilderness and the solitary place shall be glad for them; and the desert shall rejoice, and blossom as the rose. . . . And the parched ground shall become a pool, and the thirsty land springs of water (Isaiah 35:1, 7).

Every valley shall be exalted, and every mountain and hill shall be made low: and the crooked shall be made straight, and the rough places plain: and the glory of the Lord shall be revealed, and all flesh shall see it together: for the mouth of the Lord hath spoken it (Isaiah 40:4-5).

These are but two of the numerous passages we might quote from prophecy indicating the tremendous changes which will accompany the return of the Lord to the earth. When Jesus comes again at the close of the Tribulation and destroys the armies at Armageddon, the earth will also undergo physical changes unknown in the history of man.

COMPLETE REDEMPTION

When Adam sinned he did not sin alone, and when he fell he fell not as an individual, but as the federal head of God's terrestrial creation. In Adam was represented not only the whole race which should spring from him, but he was also the federal head of all that God had created on this earth and over which Adam had received dominion. When He sinned the curse of God fell not only on him and his descendants but upon the entire world. The mineral kingdom, the vegetable kingdom and the animal kingdom came under the curse of Adam's sin. When God came to curse the earth after Adam fell He said:

Cursed is the ground for thy sake.

God cursed the ground because of Adam's sin. Before sin came, the ground was perfect and one hundred per cent productive. There were no deserts and waste places.

There were no bad lands, but God "saw every thing that he had made, and, behold, it was very good." Then sin entered and the curse fell and the deserts appeared, so that today the earth does not willingly produce her wealth, but man must wrest her stores of wealth from her by constant sweat and toil while the whole creation, according to Paul in Romans 8, "groaneth and travaileth in pain together until now."

THE VEGETABLE REALM

As the earth, the soil, came under Adam's curse, so, too, all vegetation came under the curse. God said for the first time:

> Cursed is the ground for thy sake. . . . Thorns and thistles shall it bring forth to thee. . . . In the sweat of thy face shalt thou eat bread.

Weeds, insects, pests and plant disease came because of sin, and the creation was restricted in its productivity and sharply limited in its ability to satisfy the needs of man. What a struggle there is in nature today! What a toiling and sweating as the farmer fights with and for his crops against the disease and pests and weeds which make the uninterrupted battle of God's creation against the results of sin. Man calls it "the struggle for existence" and "the survival of the fittest," but God says it is the curse of sin which rests on all the earth because of Adam's sin.

THE ANIMAL REALM

The curse also affected the animals, and God said to the serpent, then the most beautiful of all the animal creation:

> Thou art cursed above all cattle, and above every beast of the field; upon thy belly shalt thou go, and dust shalt thou eat all the days of thy life.

All the animals were cursed by Adam's sin, but the serpent was cursed above them all because he had been the instrument for the introduction of sin and the curse. Before the fall there were no carnivorous animals. They

were all docile and harmless. There was no preying the
one upon the other, but all was peace and quiet and happiness in God's creation. Then sin came and changed the
nature of God's creation. Animals, birds and fish had their
natures and appetites perverted and began preying one
upon the other until truly we can say "the whole creation
groaneth and travaileth in pain together until now." Man
calls it "the struggle for existence" and "the survival of
the fittest," but God says it is creation crying for redemption.

THE LAST ADAM

As the *first* Adam brought the curse through sin, so the
Lord Jesus Christ, the *last* Adam, came to make payment
for sin and to remove the curse which lies upon creation.
In order to be a complete Redeemer, He must redeem *all*
that Adam lost. Since Adam dragged all creation with
him under the curse — the vegetable, the mineral and the
animal kingdoms — Jesus Christ, to be a perfect Redeemer, must be the Saviour of all that Adam lost. We usually
think of Christ's redemptive work as being only for fallen
mankind, but it is just as true that Jesus died on the Cross
of Calvary to redeem the earth and the plants and the
beasts and the birds and the fish from the curse. You
may think this belittles the work of Christ, that He should
not die only for men but for birds and beasts as well,
but it exalts His redemption. He is a complete Redeemer.
Presently we will show how the animal creation will be
restored at the coming again of our Lord, but first let us
consider some of the things the Bible says will happen to
this old earth and especially to the land of Palestine
when Jesus comes.

THE DESERT REDEEMED

God never made a desert. Scripture says that He made
nothing void or useless but made the entire earth to be
inhabited. Since sin made the earth barren to a large ex-
tent, when Jesus comes He will make the whole earth

once more like the Garden of Eden. The Bible makes only one exception to this, and that is the land of Moab and the marshes south of the Dead Sea as a reminder in the Millennium of what sin has done. While all the rest of the earth is like a rose garden, these places will stand as exhibits to remind us of what sin has done and they will be in sharp contrast to the glorious restoration wrought when Jesus reigns upon the earth. The prophet in Isaiah 35 speaks of this glorious time when Jesus comes. In chapter 34 of Isaiah we have a description of the Battle of Armageddon at the close of the Tribulation, and then follows Isaiah's picture of the Millennium:

> The wilderness and the solitary place shall be glad for them; and the desert shall rejoice, and blossom as the rose (Isaiah 35:1).

CHANGES IN PALESTINE

The greatest change in the land will be in Palestine. Once the most fertile land on the earth and called in Scripture the land of "milk and honey," and famed for the grapes of Eschol, during the past two and a half millenniums it has been the symbol of barrenness and the curse; two-thirds of it is jagged mountains and hills, a great part of it is wasted by the Dead Sea, and the remainder meagerly productive and dry. No wonder the skeptics scoff at the idea of Israel's going back to this land by the millions! But before they go back there will be some changes in the land. The Dead Sea will be made an inland sea teeming with life. The mountains will all be leveled, and the low miasmic marshes will be lifted up. Jerusalem will become the greatest inland harbor in the world, and the land will be covered with the most luscious vegetation in the whole earth. All this will happen by the touch of the feet of the Lord Jesus at His second coming. Consider with me a few Scripture passages which will speak for themselves and need little comment. Turn to Zechariah 14:

> Behold, the day of the Lord cometh, and thy spoil shall be divided in the midst of thee (verse 1).

In verse 2 we have a description of the Battle of Armageddon and we read in verses 3 and 4:

> Then shall the Lord go forth, and fight against those nations, as when he fought in the day of battle. And his feet shall stand in that day upon the mount of Olives, which is before Jerusalem on the east, and the mount of Olives shall cleave in the midst thereof toward the east and toward the west, and there shall be a very great valley; and half of the mountain shall remove toward the north, and half of it toward the south.

If you are a Christian, you believe this to be the word of the Lord. This teaches you that Jesus shall come again on the Mount of Olives, the same mount from which He ascended and about which the two men said, "This same Jesus . . . shall so come in like manner," and at the touch of His feet there will be a tremendous earthquake splitting the mountain from the east to the west and causing a valley from the Great Sea to the Dead Sea, so that the waters from the Mediterranean shall rush in through this channel produced by the feet of the Lord Jesus. At the same time, the Dead Sea shall be lifted from its present depression of 1,600 feet below sea level, and the two seas of the Bible will become one body of water connected by a vast channel created by the feet of King Jesus and providing Palestine with the greatest harbor in the world. On its banks will stand the city of Jerusalem, the City of Peace, where the King will reign, and all the nations shall bring their wealth and their glory into it. Listen to the word of the Lord:

> And the Lord shall be king over all the earth: in that day shall there be one Lord, and his name one. All the land shall be turned as a plain from Geba to Rimmon south of Jerusalem: and it shall be lifted up, and inhabited in her place (Zechariah 14:9, 10).

Notice the sixteenth verse which speaks of the glory of Jerusalem:

> And it shall come to pass, that every one that is left of all the nations which came against Jerusalem shall even go up from year to year to worship the King, the Lord of hosts, and to keep the feast of tabernacles.

THE LAND RESTORED

In that day the land that for centuries has lain largely waste shall be made the garden spot of the world. Palestine will be the wonder spot of the earth for fertility and beauty. Horrible as it may seem, and terrible though it be to contemplate, this restored fertility will be brought about by the bodies of millions of men who died in the Battle of Armageddon. So great will be the slaughter of the enemies of the Lord that it will take seven months to bury the dead who shall fall in the land. Many are the descriptions of this terrible battle, and we shall quote only two or three. Turn first to Revelation 14:20. This is a description of the Day of the Lord and the Battle of Armageddon, and John writes concerning that battle:

> And the winepress was trodden without the city, and blood came out of the winepress, even unto the horse bridles, by the space of a thousand and six hundred furlongs [185 miles].

So great will be the armies engaged in that battle that when the Lord comes to tread down the people in His anger there will be a stream of blood of men and horses for 185 miles drenching the land and standing in pools to the horses' bridles. The whole land will be covered by the slain. Reports coming from the Eastern European conflict already tell us that the land is being choked with slain men. Ezekiel tells us that it will take the children of Israel seven months to bury these corpses. You will find the record in Ezekiel 39, beginning at verse 11:

> And it shall come to pass in that day, that I will give unto Gog a place there of graves in Israel, the valley of the passengers on the east of the sea: and it shall stop the noses of the passengers: and there shall they bury Gog and all his multitude: and they shall call it The valley of Hamon-gog. And seven months shall the house of Israel be burying of them, that they may cleanse the land. Yea, all the people of the land shall bury them; and it shall be to them a renown the day that I shall be glorified, saith the Lord God. And they shall sever out men of continual employment, passing through the land to bury with the passengers those that remain upon the face of the earth, to cleanse it: after the end of seven months shall they search (Ezekiel 39:11-14).

You can easily see why the land will be the most fertile spot in all the world. It will be fertilized by the bodies of millions of the enemies of the Lord and the multitudes of horses. The land will be fat with the blood of God's enemies, and vegetation shall grow as it did in the Garden of Eden. Truly the desert shall "blossom as the rose."

As the curse upon the earth came through the first Adam, by the work of the last Adam and His second coming again the land, too, shall be redeemed. The earthquake will level the land. The splitting of the Mount of Olives at the touch of Jesus' feet will let the refreshing waters of the Mediterranean Sea sweep inland to the Dead Sea, making it alive, and the enriching of the land by the carcasses of the slain will enrich the soil until the land of Palestine will support countless millions in the Millennium when Abraham's seed shall be as the sand of the seashore in multitude.

EDEN RESTORED

Ezekiel, after describing the great river which shall flow through Palestine from the west to the east, gives us this graphic description in Ezekiel 47:12:

> And by the river upon the bank thereof, on this side and on that side, shall grow all trees for meat, whose leaf shall not fade [evergreen trees], neither shall the fruit thereof be consumed [everbearing trees]: it shall bring forth new fruit according to his months [twelve crops a year], because their waters they issued out of the sanctuary: and the fruit thereof shall be for meat, and the leaf thereof for medicine.

O Christian, does not your heart swell with joy within you when you think of that glad future day when war shall be no more and the curse shall be removed from nature? Best of all, Jesus, the Redeemer, will be there, and we shall see His face. All our troubles will be over and sorrow shall be no more. Reunited with our loved ones, we shall reign with Him forever and ever.

Soon we shall hear the shout "Come up hither," and we shall rise to meet Him in the air. But, O sinner, poor lost soul without Christ, you will be left behind to meet the wrath of God, to perish in the Great Tribulation and be lost forever and ever. Fly to Him now and "flee from the wrath to come." God help you and save you. He will if you will call upon Him *now*.

II

The wolf also shall dwell with the lamb, and the leopard shall lie down with the kid; and the calf and the young lion and the fatling together; and a little child shall lead them.

And the cow and the bear shall feed; their young ones shall lie down together: and the lion shall eat straw like the ox.

And the sucking child shall play on the hole of the asp, and the weaned child shall put his hand on the cockatrice' den.

They shall not hurt nor destroy in all my holy mountain: for the earth shall be full of the knowledge of the Lord, as the waters cover the sea (Isaiah 11:6-9).

We have studied together the redemption of the creation and have seen how the earth will be delivered from the bondage of the curse at the coming again of the Lord Jesus Christ. Since every realm of this earth's creation came under the curse because of the sin of the first Adam, so the last Adam will redeem every realm that fell in the first. The deserts shall become like the Garden of Eden and the waste places shall blossom like the rose. Jesus Christ is a perfect Redeemer. Since the earth and plant life and animal life came under the sentence of death and the curse because of Adam's fall, so the earth, plants and animals shall also share in the redemption provided by the Second Man who is from heaven, even the Lord Jesus.

Let us study what the Bible has to say about the redemption of the animal creation. According to Isaiah, there is a glad day coming when there will be no more ravenous beasts nor carnivorous animals, but they will all be as they were before the fall, eating only herbs and never killing and destroying one another. The classic Old Testament passage which tells us about this is found in the eleventh chapter of Isaiah. The lions, leopards and wolves will become docile and harmless, and even the asp and the cockatrice, two of the most deadly reptiles, will become harmless and will be used as pets by playing children. Many other passages in the Old Testament treat of this rebirth of the animal kingdom and it is always associated with the coming again of the Lord Jesus Christ and the setting up of the kingdom.

Turn, for instance, to the sixty-fifth chapter of Isaiah and notice the last verse of the chapter. Isaiah has been telling of the blessings of the earth when Jesus returns and the redemption of Israel in the Kingdom Age after the Tribulation and the return of the Lord. Then he describes the change which will come over the animals in that golden millennial age in these words:

> The wolf and the lamb shall feed together, and the lion shall eat straw like the bullock: and dust shall be the serpent's meat. They shall not hurt nor destroy in all my holy mountain, saith the Lord (Isaiah 65:25).

Turn to Ezekiel 34:25. Here again the prophet is extolling the blessing of the Kingdom Age when Jesus shall reign with a rod of iron and every knee shall bow to Him, when men shall have beaten "their swords into plowshares and their spears into pruninghooks," and then He says this concerning the nation of Israel:

> And I will make with them [Israel] a covenant of peace, and will cause the evil beasts to cease out of the land: and they shall dwell safely in the wilderness, and sleep in the woods (Ezekiel 34:25).

What a wonderful time that will be! How our hearts beat with glad anticipation when we think of that glorious age of one thousand years here on the earth when Jesus shall reign personally in Jerusalem, the very place where He was crucified; when Israel, who had rejected Him, shall be saved and settled in peace in the land, according to their inheritance in the twelve tribes, forever blest and safe from their enemies; when we, the Church, the bride of Christ, shall reign with Him there. The curse will be gone. The earth shall bring forth unre-

stricted and in unlimited abundance. There will be no
storms to destroy, no wars to devastate and kill, no wild
animals to tear, but all will be peace under the righteous
reign of Him who said He would come and would not
tarry. Listen again to Ezekiel as he describes that day:

> And I will make them and the places round about my
> hill a blessing; and I will cause the shower to come down
> in his season; there shall be showers of blessing. And the
> tree of the field shall yield her fruit, and the earth shall yield
> her increase, and they shall be safe in their land, and shall
> know that I am the Lord (Ezekiel 34:26-27).

The Prophet Hosea in the second chapter voices the
same glad cry as he describes that wonderful day of
Jesus' reign on the earth:

> And in that day [the day when Jesus reigns in Jerusalem
> and the nation of Israel is restored in the land, as the con-
> text shall show] will I make a covenant for them with the
> beasts of the field, and with the fowls of the heaven, and
> with the creeping things of the ground: and I will break the
> bow and the sword out of the earth, and will make them to
> lie down safely (Hosea 2:18).

Certainly no Scripture passage can be plainer than this
in showing that the blessing of redemption will include
all that fell through Adam's sin. I hear someone ask, "But
does not all this have a symbolical meaning, and must we
take it literally to mean a wolf and a lamb and a lion and
an asp? These passages are, after all, in the Old Testament, and must be spiritualized rather than taken literally."

This is the question we are asked again and again, and
in that manner men try to destroy the precious promises
of God and rob the Church of the blessed hope and Christ
of the joy of seeing the travail of His soul. Let me say
here that the miserable invention of Satan is this spiritualizing of Scripture. The curse of Christendom today
is the failure to distinguish between the Church and the
kingdom. The two are absolutely separate entities. The
Church is the body of Christ in this dispensation while
Christ is absent from earth. The kingdom is His reign on
earth. This reign was offered to Israel at His first coming

and rejected. Then the kingdom was postponed, and God revealed the mystery of the Church which is the body of Christ. Today the King is in heaven, not on the earth. The kingdom is set aside until He has finished the body and completed the Church. Then He will take the Church out of this earth and then return with her to the earth to set up the kingdom upon the earth. There can be no kingdom without the King, and as long as the King is in heaven, His kingdom will never come on earth. The kingdoms of the world today are not the kingdoms of Christ, but Scripture says that Satan is the God of this age. So we continue to pray, "Our Father which art in heaven . . . Thy kingdom come. Thy will be done on earth, as it is in heaven." That has not yet been done. Is there anyone who can look at Europe today, and at Asia, and say that God's will is being done on earth as it is in heaven? Can you look upon so-called Christian America with its hell holes and dens of vice, with its corruption in politics, government and religion, with its immorality and sin and say, "This is the kingdom, and God's will is being done on earth as it is in heaven"? Surely none can be so foolish as that. But there is a time coming when we shall cry, "The kingdom has come!" It will be at the end of the Tribulation when the seventh angel sounds his trump. Let us read Revelation 11:15:

> And the seventh angel sounded; and there were great voices in heaven, saying, The kingdoms of this world are become the kingdoms of our Lord and of his Christ; and he shall reign for ever and ever.

Let me repeat that no greater curse has ever afflicted the Church of Jesus Christ than the curse of spiritualizing Scripture, that is, making Scripture mean something other than its literal meaning. So men speak of the Church as the kingdom. They refer to Zion as the Church. They speak of Jerusalem as the bride of Christ, and of Jesus' glorious reign as His enthronement in the hearts of men, and tell us that the Millennium will result from the gradual leavening of the world through the social gospel, reform, education and the conference table. After awhile the world will be converted and wars will cease; everything will be lovely, and we will have the Millennium. But while men may teach this, there is not the remotest Scriptural evidence for such wishful thinking. It results from the miserable delusion of spiritualizing the prophecies of the Bible. Instead of spiritualizing, it is a "demonizing" of the Scriptures, for if any "spirit" has anything to do with that school of Scripture interpretation it must be an "evil spirit."

No, the Scriptures were not given to us to confuse us but rather to instruct us. Certainly God intends that we should believe His Word in all simplicity. A thousand years mean a thousand years; a wolf means a wolf; a lion means a lion. If you read your Bible that way, a child can understand it. But when you begin to symbolize Scripture it becomes utterly unintelligible. No wonder men shun the Bible and imagine it to be a book hard to understand! No wonder, I say, if God does not mean what He says. You have heard of the little girl, who, after listening to a sermon, asked her mother, "Mamma, if God doesn't mean what He says, then why doesn't He say what He means?"

Read your Bible as you would read any other book of history or fact, and it will begin to take on a new interest for you, and you will marvel at the simplicity of understanding the Bible.

NEW TESTAMENT REVELATION

Turning to the New Testament prophecies, we see that the same thing is true. Many imagine that only the Old Testament contains prophetic truth. But the New Testament is full of it, too. It teaches that the kingdom promises of blessing and peace were not fulfilled at the first coming, for they are repeated after Jesus went to heaven. Turn, for instance, to Romans 8. Here Paul, in the great redemption chapter, pauses long enough to assure us that the whole creation will share in the redemption of the day of Christ. The earth, the plants and the animals will be remembered. Read Romans 8, beginning at verse 19:

> For the earnest expectation of the creation [the word translated "creature" in this verse should be "creation." It is the same word translated "creation" in verse 22] waiteth for the manifestation of the sons of God.
> For the creation was made subject to vanity, not willingly, but by reason of him who hath subjected the same in hope.
> Because the creation itself also shall be delivered from the bondage of corruption into the glorious liberty of the children of God.
> For we know that the whole creation groaneth and travaileth in pain together until now (Rom. 8:19-22).

This entire passage refers to the creation apart from man, for in the following verse we read:

> And not only they, but ourselves also, which have the firstfruits of the Spirit, even we ourselves groan within ourselves, waiting for the adoption, to wit, the redemption of our body.

The whole creation — the earth, the trees, the birds, the fish and the animals — are waiting with earnest expectation for that glad day of redemption. How strange that man, with all his vaunted intelligence, has less sense than the animals and trees! How strange that there should be Christians who are not so wise as the beasts, and have no longing for His return.

Note a thought in each of these verses.

VERSE 19

The expectation of creation is for the manifestation of the sons of God. The word "manifestation" is really "unveiling" or "revelation." That occurs when Jesus comes back with us at the beginning of the Kingdom Age.

VERSE 20

The creature was made subject to vanity, not willingly, but by reason of another. It came under the curse through no fault of its own but because of Adam's sin. So, too, it shall be delivered without any effort by the last Adam's redemption.

VERSE 21

The creature (creation) itself shall be delivered from the bondage of corruption into the glorious liberty of the sons of God. There is no question or "maybe" here, but God says, *"It shall."*

VERSE 22

The whole creation travaileth and groaneth in pain together until now. It realizes it is under the curse. It longs for the coming of the Redeemer. It is anxiously expecting Him and waiting for Him. How piteously sad that teachers with open Bibles have been so blinded by Satan's clever wresting of Scripture by fooling them into spiritualizing the Word that they know nothing of the imminent personal return of the Lord Jesus as the only hope of the Church, and Israel and the nations and the earth and the whole creation of birds and beasts and fish and plants.

> Why speak ye not a word of the coming of the King?
> Why speak ye not of Jesus and His reign?
> Why talk about His kingdom and of its glories sing,
> And nothing of His coming back again?
>
> O hark creation's groans, how can they be assuaged?
> How can our bodies know redemptive joy?
> How can the war be ended in which we are engaged
> Except He come the lawless to destroy?
>
> Come quickly, blessed Lord, our hearts a welcome hold;
> We long to see creation's second birth;
> The promise of Thy coming to some is growing cold,
> O hasten Thy returning back to earth!
>
> Bringing back the King, bringing back the King,
> The angel choirs of heaven their hallelujahs ring;
> Bringing back the King, bringing back the King;
> Ye ransomed, let your joyous welcome ring.

III

And in that day there shall be a root of Jesse, which shall stand for an ensign of the people; to it shall the Gentiles seek: and his rest shall be glorious. And it shall come to pass in that day, that the Lord shall set his hand again the second time to recover the remnant of his people, which shall be left, from Assyria, and from Egypt, and from Pathros, and from Cush, and from Elam, and from Shinar, and from Hamath, and from the islands of the sea.

And he shall set up an ensign for the nations, and shall assemble the outcasts of Israel, and gather together the dispersed of Judah from the four corners of the earth (Isaiah 11:10-12).

How strange in the light of this and hundreds of clear revelations concerning the future restoration of the nation of Israel that there should be Christians who deny that God is going to save the nation of Israel and plant them again upon the land of Palestine and restore the kingdom of David their king. Certainly, if words mean anything at all, it is very clear from this passage that there is a time coming when God will regather all the dispersed of Israel and bring them back to the land of their fathers for peace and everlasting blessing. This passage from the eleventh chapter of Isaiah follows immediately upon the glorious description of millennial blessing when the "wolf also shall dwell with the lamb, and the leopard shall lie down with the kid," and when "they shall not hurt nor destroy in all my holy mountain." In that day, says the Lord, He will restore the nation of Israel now scattered for twenty-five hundred years throughout the hostile anti-Semitic nations. If you object and say that all this was fulfilled in the return of the Jews from Babylon under Zerubbabel and Nehemiah, you have not read the passage carefully, for under Nehemiah and Ezra and Zerubbabel, only about forty thousand returned from Babylon. But Isaiah says that God will bring them again the *second time*. Under Nehemiah it was the first time. But there is a second time coming when He will bring them from all the nations and the four corners of the earth.

GOD'S PROGRAM

God has a program for the world, the Church, the nations and for His people Israel. We have shown that God's program calls for the Church to be taken out before the terrible Day of the Lord comes. Then God will deal with the nations who have persecuted and scattered Israel, and then at the end of that time the Lord Jesus will return in person to set up His kingdom on the earth. When He comes, nature will be delivered "from the bondage of corruption." Animals will become docile and harmless and the whole world will be restored to its Edenic beauty and fruitfulness. Now that the earth, and especially the land of Palestine, has been made a Utopia and the enemies of Israel have been defeated and destroyed, the time has come for God to bring the natural seed of Abraham, Isaac and Jacob back into the land which has been theirs by covenant promise as an everlasting possession.

THE LORD'S COVENANT

The land of Palestine is the land of Israel. It has been theirs since God gave it to Abraham by promise. While many nations have had seeming possession of the land and its rightful inhabitant, Israel, has been dispersed and scattered among the nations, God has never acknowledged that the land belonged to anyone but Israel. As a result, every nation which has occupied the land of Palestine has been under the judgment of God, just as every nation which has persecuted the nation of Israel has come under the judgment of God or soon will. Israel's right to the land of Palestine goes back to the covenant of Abraham and is rooted in the irrevocable promise of a never-changing faithful God. We shall consider a few of these passages.

GENESIS 12

In Genesis 12 we have the first of numerous passages which deal with the Abrahamic covenant. In this covenant God promises to do certain things wholly and entirely independent of the conduct or future behavior of those for whom the covenant is made. It is a covenant of grace, and therefore God does it all and the fulfillment of the covenant of grace depends not on the faithfulness of man but on the faithfulness of God. The covenant God made with Abraham has to do with two things: the *seed* and the *land*. These two cannot be disassociated. The seed of Abraham belongs to the land of Israel, and the land of Israel belongs to the seed of Abraham. In Genesis 12 we read:

> Now the Lord had said unto Abram, Get thee out of thy country, and from thy kindred, and from thy father's house, unto a land that I will shew thee: and I will make of thee a great nation (Gen. 12:1-2).

Notice that God promises Abraham a land and a seed. Now turn to Genesis 13:

> And the Lord said unto Abram . . . Lift up now thine eyes, and look from the place where thou art. . . . For all the LAND which thou seest, to thee will I give it, and to thy SEED for ever (Gen. 13:14, 15).

The third statement of the covenant is in Genesis 15:

> In the same day the Lord made a covenant with Abram, saying, Unto thy SEED have I given this LAND, from the river of Egypt unto the great river, the river Euphrates (Gen. 15:18).

In this passage God defines the boundaries of the Promised Land, and you will note that the original grant to Abraham included far more than what we usually call the land of Palestine but includes all that territory stretching from the Nile River in Egypt to the Euphrates in Mesopotamia and Syria. Since Israel has never yet possessed all this and God promised it to them in the covenant of Abraham, the time must still come when all this is fulfilled.

Let us study another passage about the covenant, the Promised Land and the covenant people:

> I will establish my covenant between me and thee and thy seed after thee in their generations for an everlasting covenant, to be a God unto thee, and to thy seed after thee (Gen. 17:7).

Most Christians spiritualize this and try to apply it to the Church. But verse 8 follows verse 7, though it is never quoted by the spiritualizers. Here it is:

> And I will give unto thee, and to thy seed after thee, the LAND wherein thou art a stranger, all the land of Canaan, for an EVERLASTING possession; and I will be their God.

Many other passages might be referred to as God confirmed this covenant to Isaac and to Jacob, to Moses and to David and to Solomon. But these are enough to show that it was all of grace. There were no conditions or "if's" in the agreement. God merely promised, and will keep His promise.

THE LAW

Four hundred years after God made His covenant of grace with Abraham's seed, God made a covenant of works with the seed, Israel, at Mount Sinai. This covenant was broken because it depended on man's faithfulness and as a result Israel came under judgment, was scattered throughout the earth in the dispersion, till this day, and the land came under the curse because of Israel's sin and temporarily was occupied by strangers. It is here that many Christians fail in their understanding of the Word. They imagine that because Israel failed under the covenant of works, the law, that now God has annulled the covenant of grace with Abraham and his seed. So they tell us that God has no further dealings with Israel. The Church now is spiritual Israel, and the Abrahamic covenant applies no more to Israel but to the Church, so they say. But the fact that man was unfaithful cannot make God unfaithful. His covenant with Israel was by grace. It depended on God's faithfulness and not man's. Man always fails, but God cannot fail. One passage of Scripture will prove, I am sure, the fact that even though Israel failed under the law it did not result in their losing their place as a nation in the Abrahamic covenant. Turn to Galatians 3:17. Please follow this very carefully. Paul says:

> And this I say, that the covenant, that was confirmed before of God in Christ [the covenant with Abraham], the law, which was four hundred and thirty years after, cannot disannul, that it should make the promise of none effect. For if the inheritance be of the law, it is no more of promise: but God gave it to Abraham by promise (Gal. 3:17, 18).

Study this passage carefully and you will see the fact that a covenant of grace cannot be broken because it depends on God's faithfulness. The moment it depends on man's faithfulness it becomes a covenant of works and must fail. The covenant of grace cannot be broken because God made it with Himself, and because "he could swear by no greater, he sware by himself." Once in the covenant of grace, beloved, you can never get out, because it depends on the faithfulness of God. God made a covenant of grace with Abraham's seed, Israel. He knew they would fail. He knew they would rebel and become idolaters and reject the Son of God. But in spite of all this, God will keep His word because He gave it to Abraham by promise. Israel's disobedience calls for the chastening of the Lord and they are dispersed among the nations and under the judgment of God, but this cannot in any way prevent God from fulfilling His word in regard to the land.

THE TESTIMONY OF PROPHECY

Because Israel failed under the law, God scattered the nation and brought the curse of a broken law upon them. The nation of Babylon came against Jerusalem and they were carried away captive. But among the captives there was a remnant who still believed that God would restore the nation in the future. To these faithful ones, God sent many prophets, both while they were in captivity and after the little remnant returned. These prophets assured them that while Israel was under the curse of the law because of their sins, nevertheless, God would keep His promise and finally restore them to the land, and they could never again be disturbed or driven away. Hundreds of passages of Scripture might be quoted, but here are a few:

JEREMIAH 23:7-8:
Therefore, behold, the days come, saith the Lord, that they shall no more say, The Lord liveth, which brought up the children of Israel out of the land of Egypt; but, the Lord

liveth, which brought up and which led the seed of the house of Israel out of the north country, and from all countries whither I had driven them; and they shall dwell in their own land.

 EZEKIEL 37:21, 22, 25:

Thus saith the Lord God; Behold, I will take the children of Israel from among the heathen, whither they be gone, and will gather them on every side, and bring them into their own land: and I will make them one nation in the land upon the mountains of Israel; and one king shall be king to them all: and they shall no more be two nations, neither shall they be divided into two kingdoms any more. . . . And they shall dwell in the land that I have given unto Jacob my servant, wherein your fathers have dwelt; and they shall dwell therein, even they, and their children, and their children's children for ever: and my servant David shall be their prince for ever.

What a glorious future for this nation despised and trodden down among the nations! God says that this nation, now the object of bitterest anti-Semitism, will be brought back into the land of Palestine by God Himself, never to be driven away again. Today the nation is forsaken and the kingdom postponed while their King is in rejection. But the individuals of all nations, whether Jew or Gentile, may be saved by personal faith in Jesus Christ. God's covenant is a national covenant. No man is saved because he happens to belong to a certain race. All need to come as poor lost sinners who need cleansing by the blood of Christ. Nationally, Israel is God's covenant nation. No Gentile power will ever be able utterly to destroy them, for God has promised to restore them to the land and make them the greatest nation on the earth.

AMOS 9:13-15:

Behold, the days come, saith the Lord, that the plowman shall overtake the reaper, and the treader of grapes him that soweth seed; and the mountains shall drop sweet wine, and all the hills shall melt [what a picture of millennial blessing].

And I will bring again the captivity of my people of Israel, and they shall build the waste cities, and inhabit them; and they shall plant vineyards, and drink the wine thereof; they shall also make gardens, and eat the fruit of them.

And I will plant them [Israel] upon their land, and they shall no more be pulled up out of their land which I have given them, saith the Lord thy God.

Jesus' coming will mean much to the Church for she will be taken at the Rapture. It will mean much to the nations, for then God shall judge them in righteousness. It will mean much to creation for it also shall be delivered from the curse, but how much it will mean to the nation of Israel now scattered for these hundreds of years and persecuted and hated! The Lord says that when Jesus comes to reign He will restore the glory of the kingdom of David and Solomon, and Israel shall possess forever and be safe in the land promised to Abraham and his seed. The present European turmoil will ultimately turn to that land, the land of Israel. There the last great battle will be fought, and there the Lord will return to set up His kingdom on the earth. Until then Israel must pass through the fire until they "shall look upon him whom they have pierced and mourn over him as one that mourneth over an only begotten son" (Zechariah 12:10).

> And one shall say unto him, What are these wounds in thine hands? Then he shall answer, Those with which I was wounded in the house of my friends (Zechariah 13:6).

O that Israel, at least that remnant who have not yet abandoned the hope of their coming Messiah, might see and know that when that Messiah does come — and He will — it will be the One who came nineteen hundred years ago and shed His precious blood that "whosoever believeth in him should not perish, but have everlasting life." Let us who know Him as our Saviour pray much for Israel in her present distress, especially in Europe, and pray that the day may soon come when He who said He would come will come. "Pray for the peace of Jerusalem: they shall prosper that love thee."

CHAPTER FOUR

The Mysteries of the Kingdom

I

> And the disciples came, and said unto him, Why speakest thou unto them in parables?
> He answered and said unto them, Because it is given unto you to know the mysteries of the kingdom of heaven, but to them it is not given (Matt. 13:10-11).

Our Lord adopted a new method of teaching which begins in the thirteenth chapter of Matthew. For the first time in His ministry He spoke of the mysteries of the kingdom. Until this time in His ministry He had been speaking of the kingdom, but now He clothed His teaching in mystery and began to teach in parables. The reason for this lies in the very structure of the Gospel of Matthew.

FOUR GOSPEL RECORDS

It pleased the Holy Spirit to record the birth, life, ministry, death and Resurrection of the Lord Jesus through four human authors: Matthew, Mark, Luke and John. Each gives a distinct and separate account of the many-sided excellency of the Lord Jesus. Matthew tells us of Jesus as the King of the Jews and the Messiah of Israel. Mark tells us of Jesus as the Servant of Jehovah. Luke speaks of Jesus as the Son of Man, the Saviour of sinners, and John speaks of Jesus Christ as the Son of God. In Matthew, Jesus is the King; in Mark, He is the Servant; in Luke, He is the Son of Man; in John, He is the Son of God. Matthew, a Jew, tells us of the King of the Jews. Mark was a Roman (Mark is a Roman name), Luke was a Greek, and John is the representative of the body of Christ. Matthew, the Jew, writes of the kingdom offered to Israel. Mark, the Roman, writes to the Romans about the wonder-working Christ; Luke, the Greek physician, tells of the humanity of Christ; John tells of His deity. Matthew tells us who Jesus was — the King of Israel. Mark tells us what Jesus did, for it records His works and His miracles. Luke tells us whom He came to save. John records for us what Jesus said, for in John He is the word of God become flesh. To understand the mysteries of the kingdom it is important that this fourfold Gospel purpose be borne in mind.

THE KINGDOM GOSPEL

Matthew tells us about the King and His Gospel is fitly called the "Gospel of the Kingdom." In this book we have a picture of the King who "came unto his own, and his own received him not." He offered the kingdom to Israel but they rejected it and as a result the kingdom was postponed, Israel was rejected as a nation, and the Lord revealed the mystery age of grace in which we live today. The mysteries of the kingdom have to do with this present age of grace in which we live while the kingdom age upon earth is postponed. The first twelve chapters of Matthew tell us of the King and His offer to Israel, and after their rejection of that offer the Lord speaks about the mysteries of the kingdom. Here is an outline of the first twelve chapters of Matthew.

Chapter 1:1-17 contains the genealogy of the King of Israel. His ancestry is traced to David and then to Abraham, and no further. In Luke His ancestry is traced through the line of Mary to Adam, for Luke is talking of Jesus as the Son of Man and therefore traces Him to the first man, Adam. Matthew must establish the right of the Lord Jesus to the kingdom. In order to do this He must be proved to be, first, "of the seed of Abraham," for He must belong to the kingdom nation, and, second, He must be of the "lineage of David," for it is David's throne on which the King of Israel shall sit. This, then, Matthew must prove, and so he traces the line of Joseph, the foster father of Jesus, only to Abraham. That was enough to establish the King's right to the throne and the kingdom. Luke's genealogy is the genealogy not of a king but of the Son of Man, and therefore goes back to the beginning of man.

Matthew 1:18-25 is the record of the birth of the King. According to prophecy the King was to be born in Bethlehem, and must be born of a virgin; therefore we have Matthew's record of His birth according to Hebrew prophecy.

Matthew 2:1-23 tells of the reception of the King. We have the record of the coming of the wise men from the east. While His own people failed to own and to recognize the King, the Gentile wise men who had seen His star believed and came to Him to worship Him and present Him with kingly gifts — gold and frankincense and myrrh. It is a prophetic picture of what is to follow, for "he came unto his own, and his own received him not. But as many as received him, to them gave he power to become the sons of God." The King is here rejected by His own people, but owned by those who were afar off.

Matthew 3 tells of the herald of the King. The King must be announced and introduced, and so we have the record of John the Baptist, the King's herald, who declares himself to be —

> The voice of one crying in the wilderness, Prepare ye the way of the Lord, make his paths straight.

A potentate must be announced and heralded. If the President were to come to your city, the police would clear the streets and the coming of the President would be preceded and accompanied by a cordon of soldiers preparing the way. Thus our King came the first time, and when He comes again He will be preceded by Elijah the prophet, the John the Baptist of the second coming.

Matthew 4:16-17 tells of the preparation of the King. It records His temptation in the wilderness. He is now to prove that He is able to be a King. The first Adam fell under the onslaught of the devil. He fell from his kingdom, for Adam was created to be a king. God gave him dominion over all the works of His hands but he fell and became a slave to sin and to death. Then the last Adam comes, and He is to prove that He is the Master of the enemy. He meets him on the same basis that the first Adam did, but with another result. He conquers and comes forth victorious. He has proved his worthiness to be the King.

In Matthew 4:18-25 we read about the King's selection of His cabinet. He calls Peter, James, John and Andrew, and the tenth chapter adds eight more to this number. They are the ones who shall sit upon twelve thrones judging the twelve tribes of Israel when the kingdom is set up. We now come to three chapters (Matthew 5, 6 and 7) which you all know as the Sermon on the Mount, probably the most misunderstood and misrepresented chapters in the Bible. In these three chapters Jesus gives the constitution and bylaws of the kingdom He had come to offer. It is the rule of the kingdom and contains the laws which will govern the subjects of the King during His reign upon the earth. It contains the requisites for membership in the kingdom, in the Beatitudes. It describes the subjects as salt and light in the world. It records the law of the kingdom, and chapter 6 describes the worship of the kingdom and records the so-called Lord's Prayer which is really the disciples' kingdom prayer. Chapter 7 tells of the permanence of the kingdom.

Having given the constitution of the kingdom, Jesus in Matthew 8 and 9 presents the credentials of the King. In these two chapters we have a record of miracles and signs and wonders. He heals the sick, stills the waves, casts out demons, gives sight to the blind, and proves that He is the Master of the natural and the supernatural and performs those miracles which are for the Kingdom Age, but have been misapplied by so many in this age because they have confused this age of grace with the kingdom.

Matthew 10 continues the record. Having presented His credentials by the working of countless miracles, He now offers the kingdom to the nation. He sends twelve men with the message: "The kingdom of heaven is at hand." He does not say, "The kingdom of heaven is here." That would come only if they received the King. Until they accept Him the kingdom cannot come. So the message of the offer is this: "The kingdom of heaven is at hand." It is here for you, right at hand if you will receive Him as King, but they received Him not. In the very next chapter, Matthew 11, we have the record of His rejection by the leaders of the nation. The chapter closes with the pronouncement of woes upon the nation and the land.

Matthew 12 tells of the sin of blasphemy against the Holy Ghost. From this point on, Jesus turns from them and begins to reveal an entirely new truth which had never before been revealed. This new truth we find in Matthew 13 under the name of the mysteries of the kingdom. He now clothes His teaching in parables, and speaks of mysteries which some can understand and others cannot see. Our Lord now reveals that in God's eternal plan He knew that when the King would come to offer the kingdom the first time, He would not be received, and so God had a secret in His plan. That secret was that during the time of the postponement of the kingdom and the rejection of the nation, He would gather out another people, a heavenly people, called the Church, the body of Christ and the bride of Christ. This was a plan which had not been revealed before. The believing Israelite believed that when Messiah would come He would set up the throne in Jerusalem, deliver Israel from the cruel Roman oppressor and begin the glad millennial reign for which every believing Israelite was yearning. He knew nothing of the intervening age of grace and the gathering out of

the body of Christ, while Israel would be in dispersion,
until this secret plan of God was completed. That plan is
called the mystery of the kingdom of heaven.

"KINGDOM" AND "MYSTERY"

There is a great difference between the kingdom of
heaven and the mystery of the kingdom of heaven. The
kingdom of heaven is the literal reign of the Lord Jesus
Christ on this earth, when He shall sit on the throne of
His father David in Jerusalem. To speak of the Church
as the kingdom is utterly unscriptural. To call the Church
"Zion" and "Jerusalem" and "spiritual Israel" has no
foundation in Scripture. The kingdom of heaven is the
reign of heaven's King on the earth. This Jesus offered
to the nation of Israel when He came the first time, but
they rejected it and He went to the Cross. Until Israel
owns her King, we are living in the age of the *mystery*
of the kingdom of heaven. All the revelations concerning
this age of grace are called in Scripture a *mystery* —
mysteries because they were not fully revealed until the
Church Age of grace, mysteries because they are understood only by those who belong by virtue of regeneration
to the mystery body of Christ, and to all others they remain mysteries and foolishness.

ALL IS MYSTERY

There are many mysteries mentioned in the New Testament concerning this intervening age between the Lord's
first coming and His second coming. That is the period
of time during which the King is absent from the kingdom and His kingdom people, Israel, are in rejection also.
Everything which happens during that absence is called
a *mystery*. We have time only to name them, and then we
shall define what the mystery really is, why Jesus spoke
in parables and then discuss the individual mysteries in
detail.

1. The mystery of Israel's rejection (Romans 11:25).
2. The mystery of the body of Christ (Ephesians 3).

3. The mystery of the Bride of Christ, the Church (Ephesians 5:31-32).
4. The mystery of the Incarnation of the Son of God (I Timothy 3:16).
5. The mystery of iniquity, the false king (II Thessalonians 2).
6. The mystery of Babylon, the false messiah's church (Revelation 17).
7. The mystery of the Rapture of the Church (I Corinthians 15:51).
8. The mystery of the seven stars in Christ's hand (Revelation 1).
9. The mystery of the new birth (Colossians 1:27-28).

The last of these mysteries, the mystery of the new birth, is the first essential. All the other tremendous truths about God's program for Israel, the Rapture of the Church and the coming of the mystery man, the Antichrist, will remain mysteries to you until you have experienced the mysterious power of regeneration. Jesus said, "Ye must be born again," "Verily, verily, I say unto thee, except a man be born again, he cannot *see* the kingdom of God." Until you have accepted the Lord Jesus as your personal Saviour you can never understand the Scriptures or know the mysteries, for mysteries in the Word are those things which only those who know Christ can understand. Jesus said that God had "hid these things from the wise and prudent, and hast revealed them unto babes." You must first become a babe before you can understand God's plan and Word. That means you must be born into the family of God.

In John 3:16 we read:

> God so loved the world, that he gave his only begotten Son, that whosoever believeth in him should not perish, but have everlasting life.

God so loved that He gave. God offers you life, but you must receive that life, for in John 1:12 and 13 we read:

> But as many as received him, to them gave he power to become the sons of God, even to them that believe on his name: which were born, not of blood, nor of the will of the flesh, nor of the will of man, but of God.

My friend, have you been born again? That is the first question to settle before you can understand the mysteries of God. It is so simple. Only believe. Believe that Jesus died for you and receive Him by faith. God will open your eyes.

II

> For I would not, brethren, that ye should be ignorant of this mystery, lest ye should be wise in your own conceits; that blindness in part is happened to Israel, until the fullness of the Gentiles be come in. And so all Israel shall be saved: as it is written, There shall come out of Sion the Deliverer, and shall turn away ungodliness from Jacob; for this is my covenant unto them, when I shall take away their sins (Romans 11:25-27).

God does not place a premium upon ignorance of the Word of God and the plan of His dealings with men. The Lord has given us the revelation of His Word to instruct us and to inform us of His eternal plan regarding Israel, His nation, the Church, His bride and the nations of the Gentiles. This plan of God is a mystery to those who are unenlightened by the Holy Spirit but perfectly plain to those who have experienced the mysterious new birth. Paul says, "I would not, brethren, that ye should be ignorant of this mystery, lest ye should be wise in your own conceits." The things he speaks of have to do with a mystery and that mystery is God's dealings in this present age with His covenant people, Israel.

The word "mystery" in Scripture comes from the Greek word *mysterion*. This Greek word comes from the root word *muo*, which means literally "to shut the mouth." To shut the mouth is to keep a secret. That is the basic meaning of the word "mystery" in the New Testament. It is the revelation of a secret which had not been known before and one which is known only by a certain few and is kept hidden from all others. The word was originally applied to the members of a secret religious order. **Only** those who had been initiated into the order, knew the password and were familiar with the secret code, knew the mysteries of the order. To all others it was just "so much Greek." The things called "mysteries" in the **New** Testament by the Lord Jesus and the apostles are secrets to all except those who have been initiated into the family of God by the blood of Jesus Christ. They only know the password and they alone know the secret code by faith; to all others these great truths are hidden and misunderstood. We have mentioned nine of the mysteries. Let us consider the mystery of Israel's blindness until the fullness of the Gentiles be come in.

A COVENANT PEOPLE

Some two thousand years before Christ came, God made a covenant with His servant Abraham. This covenant had to do with two things: a seed and a land where the seed was to dwell and which He gave to Abraham's seed as an everlasting possession. This covenant was repeated seven times to Abraham and in each case it promised Abraham that the land of Palestine was the irrevocable inheritance of his seed, the descendants of Abraham through Isaac and through Jacob and known to us as the children of Israel, or Israelites. God summarizes this covenant in Genesis 17:7-8:

> And I will establish my covenant between me and thee and thy seed after thee in their generations for an everlasting covenant, to be a God unto thee, and to thy seed after thee.
> And I will give unto thee, and to thy seed after thee, the land wherein thou art a stranger, all the land of Canaan, for an everlasting possession; and I will be their God.

This was the promise of God to Abraham in behalf of himself and his seed. At the time when Christ came, this land was under the heel of the Roman despot. The seed of Abraham were vassals of a Gentile power because of their disobedience to the law of God. To the believing remnant in Israel, the coming of their Messiah, the **King** of Israel, would mark the day of their liberation and emancipation, and they believed that when He came the kingdom would be restored to Israel and the unconditional covenant God made with Abraham would find its fulfillment. All the prophets had spoken of this golden age, and the believing remnant believed it would come. Hence, when Jesus came they expected Him to set up the kingdom. The disciples believed this for they asked Him repeatedly, "Wilt thou at this time restore the kingdom?" They vied among each other for places of honor in the kingdom. Even after Jesus' death and Resurrection they were still expecting Him to set up that kingdom, for we hear them asking on Mount Olivet:

> Lord, wilt thou at this time restore again the kingdom to Israel? (Acts 1:6).

To this question Jesus gave His answer. He did not say, "You are mistaken about a literal kingdom for Israel. I am now going to make the Church the kingdom of heaven. I am all through with Israel as a nation. You must take all those Old Testament prophecies concerning Israel's kingdom and spiritualize them to make the Church spiritual Israel, and apply all the kingdom promises to the Church." No! He said nothing of the kind. Instead, He assured them that God in His own time would "restore again the kingdom of Israel" but this was not the time. And so He answered:

> It is not for you to know the times or the seasons, which the Father hath put in his own power (Acts 1:7).

Then He added:

> But ye shall receive power, after that the Holy Ghost is come upon you: and ye shall be witnesses unto me both in Jerusalem, and in all Judaea, and in Samaria, and unto the uttermost part of the earth (Acts 1:8).

Jesus now spoke of the mystery age, while the kingdom is postponed, during which the Gospel is to go into all the earth. The rest of the book of Acts records the fulfillment of this commission, for the apostles did begin to preach in Jerusalem, then in Judaea, then in Samaria and

finally to the ends of the earth. All this was in answer to
the question:

> Lord, wilt thou at this time restore again the kingdom to
> Israel?

"No!" said the Lord, "not at this time." He did not say
that it would never be done, but "Not at this time." God
will reveal the mystery age between this time and the
final establishment of the kingdom. The kingdom is to
be set aside for a time and the Church will be called out
in the interim. This was the mystery the Israelite before
the Cross did not know, and therefore, it is called the
mystery. Even John the Baptist did not see this. He had
preached, "The kingdom of heaven is at hand," and probably expected a prominent place in that kingdom. Then
he had been imprisoned and had heard of the waning
popularity of the King, and he began to doubt also. He
accordingly sent his disciples to Jesus with the question:
"Art thou he that should come? or look we for another?"
The kingdom was set aside and, instead, the Holy Spirit
came on Pentecost. After awhile not only Jews but Gentiles were invited into the Church. Paul and the apostles
began preaching not a kingdom but a body, the Church.
This the Jew could not understand. He imagined that the
Messiah Christ would set up a kingdom, and that kingdom
would be for Israel, not a Gentile kingdom. They had to
settle this and they called a council in Jerusalem to discuss this question. We have the record in Acts 15. There
was much disputing as to whether the Gentiles could come
into the Church without keeping the law and being cir-
cumcised. That meant they had to become Jews, for they
were still thinking in terms of the kingdom. The questions that bothered them were: "If God is now calling out
a Church, then what about all the promises of God to
Abraham and through the prophets and to David concerning an earthly kingdom in Palestine for David? Must
all that be forgotten? Has God changed His mind? Will

there be no kingdom, and is God all through with the
nation of Israel, and is the Church now taking her place
as spiritual Israel?" Those certainly were legitimate
questions, since the mystery of Israel's rejection was not
yet fully revealed. James gave the answer. Follow it
closely in Acts 15:13. Here we read:

> And after they had held their peace, James answered,
> saying, Men and brethren, hearken unto me: Simeon [Peter]
> hath declared how God at the first did visit the Gentiles, to
> take out of them a people for his name.

Here is the key. The kingdom will be set up for Israel
but first, God has a mystery to fulfill, and that mystery is
the taking out of the Gentiles "a people for his name."
This people, we know, is the Church, the body of Christ
and the bride of the Lamb. Even though He does that,
this does not mean that God will not keep His kingdom
promise, or that this is contrary to the prophets who said
that the Messiah would set up the promised kingdom of
Israel, for James adds in Acts 15:15, 16:

> And to this agree the words of the prophets; as it is
> written, After this I will return, and will build again the
> tabernacle of David, which is fallen down; and I will build
> again the ruins thereof, and I will set it up.

Note carefully the revelation here. James says that
first in this dispensation God is gathering out His Church
from among the Gentiles. While this mystery was not
fully revealed in the Old Testament, nor understood by
Israel, it did not mean that the prophets were wrong and
that there would be no kingdom. On the contrary, James
says, "To this agree the words of the prophets. . . After
this I will return." "After this I will return." After what?
After He has taken out of the Gentiles a people for His
Name. When He has done that, He will return and will
set up the kingdom of David on the earth. Israel had
expected Jesus to do this at His first coming, but did not
know the mystery that between the first coming and second coming the kingdom would be postponed and God
would call out His Church, and after that He would re-

turn to fulfill every covenant promise made to Israel and gloriously prophesied by the prophets of old.

THE MYSTERY OF THE KINGDOM

Israel is to be set aside until God's mystery age is finished. We read in Romans 11:25, 26:

> For I would not, brethren, that ye should be ignorant of this mystery, lest you should be wise in your own conceits; that blindness in part is happened to Israel, until the fulness of the Gentiles be come in.
> And so all Israel shall be saved: as it is written.

Yes, God will keep His promises. Not one shall fail. The Israel of Paul's day could not understand how God could forget His kingdom promises and call out a Church. Those who call themselves "spiritual Israel" are as blind as natural Israel. They, too, tell us that God is all through with Israel and the Jew. They tell us that the Church has taken the place of Israel, and that they are spiritual Israel. By a process of "spiritualizing" of the Scriptures, which is nearer a "demonizing," than spiritualizing, they tell us that God is all through with His ancient people Israel, that Jesus will never set up a literal kingdom on the earth and that all the Old Testament promises to Israel must be applied to the Church. They do not understand the mystery. It is, according to Paul, "ignorance" of the mystery of God's plan.

Israel will be restored, and the kingdom promised to Abraham, David, Solomon and Christ will be set up on the earth. I shall give only a few of the prophesies touching this truth. The Lord predicted the scattering of the nation in the days of Moses when He said in Leviticus 26:

> And I will scatter you among the heathen, and will draw out a sword after you: and your land shall be desolate, and your cities waste. . .
> And yet for all that, when they be in the land of their enemies, I will not cast them away, neither will I abhor them utterly, and to break my covenant with them: for I am the Lord their God. But I will for their sakes remember the covenant of their ancestors, whom I brought forth out of the land of Egypt (Leviticus 26:33, 44, 45).

In Deuteronomy 30 we read:

The Lord thy God will turn thy captivity, and have compassion upon thee, and will return and gather thee from all the nations, whither the Lord thy God hath scattered thee. . . . And the Lord thy God will bring thee into the land which thy fathers possessed, and thou shalt possess it (Deut. 30:3, 5).

In Isaiah 11 we read:

The Lord shall set his hand again the second time to recover the remnant of his people, which shall be left, from Assyria . . . Egypt . . . Pathros . . . Cush . . . Elam . . . Shinar . . . Hamath . . . and from the islands of the sea (Isaiah 11:11).

Jeremiah 23:7 tells us:

Therefore, behold, the days come, saith the Lord, that they shall no more say, The Lord liveth, which brought up the children of Israel out of the land of Egypt, but the Lord liveth, which brought up and which led the seed of the house of Israel out of the north country, and from all countries whither I had driven them; and they shall dwell in their own land.

Jeremiah 33:25, 26 declares:

Thus saith the Lord; If my covenant be not with day and night, and if I have not appointed the ordinances of heaven and earth; then will I cast away the seed of Jacob, and David my servant, so that I will not take any of his seed to be rulers over the seed of Abraham, Isaac, and Jacob: for I will cause their captivity to return, and have mercy on them.

"Hath God cast away his people? God forbid . . . God hath not cast away his people which he foreknew" (Romans 11:1, 2).

For I would not, brethren, that ye should be ignorant of this mystery . . . that blindness in part is happened to Israel, until the fulness of the Gentiles be come in.

In connection with the mystery of the fullness of the Gentiles I suggest that you read carefully the third chapter of Ephesians. It gives the key to the understanding of this mystery. What a glorious future lies ahead for the believer! One of these days the last member of the body of Christ will be won for Him. Then Jesus shall come to take out the Church. After the brief reign of the mystery of iniquity, Christ will return with the Church to set up the kingdom, to restore Israel to her rightful place among the nations and then —

> Christ shall have dominion
> Over land and sea;
> Earth's remotest regions
> Shall His empire be.

III

For this cause I Paul, the prisoner of Jesus Christ for you Gentiles, if ye have heard of the dispensation of the grace of God which is given me to you-ward: how that by revelation he made known unto me the mystery; (as I wrote afore in few words, whereby when ye read, ye may understand my knowledge in the mystery of Christ.)

Which in other ages was not made known unto the sons of men, as it is now revealed unto his holy apostles and prophets by the Spirit.

That the Gentiles should be fellow heirs, and of the same body, and partakers of his promise in Christ by the gospel. . .

And to make all men see what is the fellowship of the mystery, which from the beginning of the world hath been hid in God, who created all things by Jesus Christ (Ephesians 3:1-6, 9).

Paul tells us in these few but informative words that he had been chosen of God to make known a revelation which in other ages was not understood, but which God had hidden until this particular time. Paul did not receive this information from the Scriptures, but it was given to him by special revelation of God. This revelation Paul calls "the mystery, which from the beginning of the world hath been hid in God" — a mystery which in other ages was not made known unto the sons of men as it is now revealed by His holy apostles and prophets by the Spirit.

THE MYSTERY OF THE BODY

This mystery, this new revelation which Paul received here, has to do with a new thing which God purposed to do after Pentecost, that is, after the coming of the Holy Spirit. We have seen that the rejection of the nation of Israel was a mystery not known to the Old Testament saints. They believed that when the Messiah came He would immediately set up His kingdom. They knew nothing of the fact that between the first coming of the King and the second coming there would be an age of grace, called the mystery age. Paul calls it the "dispensation of the grace of God" in Ephesians 3:2. During this dispensation of the grace of God, the Church is being formed into one body, and when that body is completed, it will be caught up to meet the Lord in the air to be forever with the Lord.

UNKNOWN TO PROPHETS

This truth concerning the Church as a body of believers entirely separate from the nation of Israel, a heavenly people instead of an earthly people, was unknown to God's people before Pentecost. We have seen that the apostles knew nothing of it before the Cross or even after the Cross until God gave it by revelation to them. You may search diligently but you will find no Church in the Old Testament. Those who contend that the Church started in Eden with Adam do not understand the Church as the body of Christ. Those who would begin the Church with Abraham and make the covenant God made with Abraham the new covenant in His blood have not yet grasped the mystery of the Body. They are still afflicted with Israel's blindness. The Church of Jesus Christ was born on the day of Pentecost. Jesus, in speaking of His Church, says in Matthew 16: "Upon this rock [referring to Himself] I will build my church." He does not say, "I have been building," or "I will continue to build My Church," but He says definitely in the future tense, "I *will build* my church."

THE SPIRIT'S BIRTHDAY

Besides calling Pentecost the "birthday" of the Church, we may also call it the "birthday of the Holy Spirit," not meaning by this, of course, that the Spirit was born on this day as beginning His existence, but it was that day in which He entered a body and incarnated Himself in the Church of Jesus Christ which is His body. In the same way we speak of the birthday of Jesus Christ, nineteen hundred years ago. By this we do not mean that

Jesus Christ began His existence, for He always was, but then He took up His abode in a body, when that body was born. In the very same way the Holy Spirit formed the body of the Church on the day of Pentecost and, therefore, that day can be 'called the birthday of the Spirit. This new work of the Spirit in forming a mystical body composed of all believers was already suggested when the Spirit formed the physical body in the womb of the Virgin Mary.

ONE BODY

Until Pentecost God had left the nations and the Gentiles alone. He was dealing under the law with only one nation: the nation of Israel. After they had rejected the claims of the King, God set them aside and began a new work in which there were no national distinctions. This body, which God is forming today, is composed of men and women from all nations, whether Jew or Gentile, whether white or black, whether bond or free, rich or poor. The middle wall of partition which separated Jew and Gentile is broken down and now "whosoever will may come." God is now dealing with the individual in calling out His body. In a previous message we pointed out that the work of the Holy Spirit in this day and age is to call out from among the Gentiles "a people for his name." There is not one verse in Scripture which states that this age will end in a revival that will see all men saved. There is nothing in the Bible to give the faintest encouragement to the unbiblical teaching that the so-called "leaven" of the Gospel will finally permeate society and the teachings of Christ, the Golden Rule and the Sermon on the Mount will so change the hearts of men that they will all come to know Christ and then the Millennium will be here. This has never been the program of God. Instead, according to the words of James in Acts 15, He is calling *out* a people. The very word "church" in the Greek means a "called out company." The word is *ecclesia,* from two other words: *ek,* meaning "out" and *kaleo,* meaning "to call." God is calling out a few here and a few there to make up the body of His elect Church. There is no wholesale salvation. At Pentecost five thousand were saved but this was only "a drop in the bucket" compared with the tens of thousands who were celebrating the Feast of Pentecost in Jerusalem on that day.

HAS GOD FAILED?

Many people believe the Gospel has failed because after nineteen hundred years of Gospel preaching the world is yet unconverted, yea, seems to be farther from God now than ever before. They imagine that something must be wrong because nineteen hundred years after the Prince of Peace came we are engaged in the greatest and most demoniacal war of all time. The Postmillennialist who had been preaching a better world getting better and better by the preaching of a so-called gospel and education and reform has abandoned his dream and taken refuge in the rickety and still more untenable theory of Amillennialism. This results from his failure to understand the mystery of the body of Christ. It was never God's program to convert the world in this dispensation. On the contrary, the Bible teaches clearly that this age will end in apostasy and wickedness, war and destruction. God's program does not call for conversion of the world *now,* but the opposite. That is the very point of James' speech at the first council at Jerusalem. Though we have quoted him before, look at his words again:

> Simeon hath declared how God at the first did visit the Gentiles, to take out of them a people for his name (Acts 15:14).

This verse says nothing about the conversion of the world. Rather, He is taking out some from among the Gentiles. These are the members of the body of Christ. They are the mystery members, from every tribe, race and nation, who by faith in Jesus' shed blood are made partakers of His grace and constitute that comparatively small group of true born-again believers in every age. Then He tells us that after that body has been taken out He will return.

> After this I will return, and will build again the tabernacle of David, which is fallen down; and I will build again the ruins thereof, and I will set it up (Acts 15:16).

Following the taking out of the Church, the Lord will restore the kingdom of David and Israel, and then will come world revival and conversion, as is plainly stated in the next verse:

> That the residue of men might seek after the Lord, and all the Gentiles, upon whom my name is called, saith the Lord, who doeth all these things. Known unto God are all his works from the beginning of the world (Acts 15:17-18).

How strange that men with open Bibles should still dream of a better world and a federation of nations and universal peace without the re-establishment of the kingdom after the personal return of the King.

THE LAST DAYS

Volumes could be written to show the Bible teaches gradual deterioration in this dispensation rather than the golden age of peace of which men dream. Jesus said of the last days of this dispensation:

> Take heed that no man deceive you. For many shall come in my name, saying, I am Christ; and shall deceive many. And ye shall hear of wars and rumours of wars . . . For nation shall rise against nation, and kingdom against kingdom: and there shall be famines, and pestilences, and earthquakes, in divers places.

Paul, in writing to Timothy, warns him against the latter days and tells him that it will be a time of great peril:

> Now the Spirit speaketh expressly, that in the latter times some shall depart from the faith, giving heed to seducing spirits, and doctrines of devils; speaking lies in hypocrisy; having their conscience seared with a hot iron (I Timothy 4:1, 2).

In his second epistle he expresses the same idea with added emphasis that we might not be dismayed by the increase of evil and wickedness in the world but might know the program of God. He says to Timothy and to us:

> This know also, that in the last days perilous times shall
> come. For men shall be lovers of their own selves, cove-
> tous, boasters, proud, blasphemers, disobedient to parents,
> unthankful, unholy, without natural affection, trucebreakers,
> false accusers, incontinent, fierce, despisers of those that are
> good, traitors, heady, highminded, lovers of pleasures more
> than lovers of God; having a form of godliness, but denying
> the power thereof (II Timothy 3:1-5).

I ask you, friend, is this a picture of a world converted
to Christ? Was Paul wrong when he gave this photo-
graph of the last days? Does the Bible teach the foolish
doctrine that the race will get better and better until
universal peace and Christianity are ushered in? I tell
you, my friend, this idealistic teaching of a social gospel
which holds before men the will-o'-the-wisp of a better
world through the social gospel, education, reform and
legislation is a snare and a delusion. God has a program
of His own and happy is he who leaves the ethereal vapor-
izing of man's vain philosophical hopes, and believes the
program of God and orders his life accordingly. If you
refuse to believe God's Word then all this must remain
for you a mystery. It is all foolishness to you.

THE PROGRAM

Here is God's program as given in His Word. During
this present dispensation the King is in heaven. Israel is
set aside as a nation but preserved for her future place in
the kingdom. During the interval of the King's absence,
the Holy Spirit is gathering from among all nations a
Church, composed of all who accept Jesus Christ as
Saviour by faith. When the number which God foreknew
would believe have been called out into that body, the
Lord will return from heaven and take His body home,
together with all the Old Testament saints who have died
in the faith. The dead in Christ shall all rise at His voice
as He shouts from the air; the living believers will be
changed and joined with the resurrected ones who rise to
meet the Lord in the air. While we are with the Lord in
the air, He will judge the nations of the earth, and will

pass Israel through the fires of the Great Tribulation, to purify them and fit them to enter into the kingdom He is about to set up. At the end of seven years He will come back with His Church, now His bride, and He will destroy the wicked nations. Israel will be converted and accept her Messiah, and then Jesus will set up the kingdom on earth in fulfillment of all the promises made to Abraham, Isaac, Jacob, David and by the mouth of all the prophets.

THE NEXT NUMBER ON THE PROGRAM

The next number on God's program is the coming of the Lord Jesus to take out His Church. Everything Jesus said concerning the last days is beginning to be fulfilled. The graphic description of Paul to Timothy which we read is actually the description of the very days of violence, immorality and vice in which you and I are living. Soon the shout will come from the air and Jesus will come. Every sleeping saint shall be raised and every believer alive shall be changed. Thank God, I am ready for that day, for I am saved by His grace and have been "called out." Friend, are *you* ready? You have heard the invitation. You have been told God's program. It need be a mystery to you no longer. Before another day it may be too late, but now you can still look to Jesus and "flee from the wrath to come." God help you to do it now. It is so simple. Just believe God's Word and trust His Son Jesus Christ for salvation *now*, and you will know the glad truth that you are a member of His body and are forever safe in His fold.

IV

Behold, I shew you a mystery; We shall not all sleep, but we shall all be changed, in a moment, in the twinkling of an eye, at the last trump: for the trumpet shall sound, and the dead shall be raised incorruptible; and we shall be changed. For this corruptible must put on incorruption, and this mortal must put on immortality. So when this corruptible shall have put on incorruption and this mortal shall have put on immortality, then shall be brought to pass the

saying that is written, Death is swallowed up in victory (I
Corinthians 15:51-54).

"Behold, I shew you a mystery." That is the statement
with which Paul begins this closing section of the
fifteenth chapter of First Corinthians, the great resurrection chapter of the Bible. He introduces the passage with
the word "behold." Someone has said that the word "behold" in the Scriptures is the "Stop, Look, and Listen"
sign of the Bible. It always calls for special attention
and directs our attention to a truth of unusual importance. "Behold, I shew you a mystery." A mystery in
Scripture, as you know, is a truth that was not revealed
fully before and is made clear only to those who know the
"code" of the Word and have been initiated into the fraternity of the sons of God by faith in the Lord Jesus
Christ. We have dealt with a number of these mysteries
which have to do with this present age between the ascen-
sion of the King into heaven and His second coming again
in glory. This age was a mystery to the Old Testament
saint. It was the secret part of God's plan. The Old
Testament Israelite expected the kingdom to be set up at
the coming of the Messiah, but instead He was rejected,
went to the Cross and, instead of the kingdom, we have
now the Church Age and the calling out of the body of
Christ, and this period of time is known as the mystery
of the kingdom of heaven. The kingdom itself is postponed until this secret part of God's plan in calling out
the Church is completed.

THE CHURCH A MYSTERY

The first mystery we studied was the mystery of Israel's
rejection and the postponement of the kingdom on earth.
Then we studied the mystery of the body of Christ. This
body of Christ now being formed by the ministry of the
Holy Spirit will one day be completed, and then the
Church will become the bride of Christ. She will be
caught up at the Rapture when Jesus returns in the air to

awaken all the dead saints and change all living believers and take her out before the mystery of iniquity is revealed on the earth in the person of the Superman of Sin, the Antichrist. The New Testament has much to say about this "catching away" of the Church at the end of this age of grace but it was never clearly revealed in the Old Testament. That is why it is called a mystery, and so Paul says, "Behold I shew you a *mystery*."

THE IMMINENT EVENT

One of these days the Lord Jesus Christ who was born in a stable in Bethlehem and laid in a manger will come back for His Church. The same Jesus who walked the dusty roads of Palestine, healing the sick, raising the dead and casting out demons, is coming back again to raise all the believing dead and to heal the brokenhearted and cast the archdemon, the devil, into the bottomless pit. There can be no question about the teaching of Scripture concerning this event, but the order of the events was a mystery. The second coming of Christ in glory was no mystery to the Old Testament believer and prophets, for the prophecies are replete with descriptions of the coming of the Lord in glory to set up His kingdom; but they knew nothing of the two aspects of His coming; that is, that first the Lord would come *for* His Church to take her out of this world before the Tribulation, and then come *with* His Church to reign on the earth. The first stage of His coming, which we call the Rapture, is the mystery, and this is the event that Paul refers to when he says, "Behold, I shew you a mystery."

THE DEAD IN CHRIST SHALL RISE FIRST

Scripture gives the details and the order of this blessed hope. First the Lord Jesus will descend from heaven with a shout, accompanied by the archangel and his hosts; the trumpet will be blown and all the dead in Christ shall arise, followed by the instantaneous translation of living believers with the resurrected saints. The classic passage dealing with this truth is I Thessalonians 4:13-18:

> But I would not have you to be ignorant, brethren, concerning them which are asleep, that ye sorrow not, even as others which have no hope.
>
> For if we believe that Jesus died and rose again, even so also them which sleep in Jesus will God bring with him.
>
> For this we say unto you by the word of the Lord, that we which are alive and remain unto the coming of the Lord shall not prevent [precede] them which are asleep.
>
> For the Lord himself shall descend from heaven with a shout, with the voice of the archangel, and with the trump of God: and the dead in Christ shall rise first: then we which are alive and remain shall be caught up together with them in the clouds, to meet the Lord in the air: and so shall we ever be with the Lord.
>
> Wherefore comfort one another with these words.

Certainly this passage needs no exposition. It is so clear and definite that a child can understand it. All you need to do with a passage like this is *believe* it. A friend said to me some time ago when I quoted that passage, "But, Doctor, what does that mean?" and I answered:

> The Lord himself shall descend from heaven with a shout, with the voice of the archangel, and with the trump of God: and the dead in Christ shall rise first: then we which are alive and remain shall be caught up together with them in the clouds, to meet the Lord in the air: and so shall we ever be with the Lord.

"That is what it means," said I, but he answered, "Yes, yes, that is what it says, but what is the interpretation?" "Oh, I see your point," I replied. "You want the theological interpretation of the passage. Well, here it is":

> The Lord himself shall descend from heaven with a shout, with the voice of the archangel, and with the trump of God: and the dead in Christ shall rise first: then we which are alive and remain shall be caught up together with them in the clouds, to meet the Lord in the air: and so shall we ever be with the Lord.

Brother, you do not have to explain or expound that. It means just what it says. The Lord is coming again. That was the promise He left us:

> Let not your heart be troubled: ye believe in God, believe also in me. In my Father's house are many mansions: if it were not so, I would have told you. I go to prepare a place for you. And if I go and prepare a place for you, I will come again, and receive you unto myself; that where I am, there ye may be also (John 14:1-3).

This was our Lord's parting message before He left His disciples, and all we need to do is believe it. The first message our blessed Lord sent back when He had gone to heaven was the same blessed assurance of His return, immediately after the clouds of heaven swallowed up the Lord when He ascended from Mt. Olivet. He sent back two men in white apparel which also said:

> Ye men of Galilee, why stand ye gazing up into heaven? this same Jesus, which is taken up from you into heaven, shall so come in like manner as ye have seen him go into heaven (Acts 1:11).

THE ORDER

Here, then, is the order of events at the coming of the Lord. First, at the shout of the Lord as He descends into the air according to His promise, all the dead who have died in faith shall arise with resurrection bodies — painless, sinless, deathless, incorruptible bodies. As these dead come from their graves, the living believers will join them and be changed in a moment into the likeness of Christ with their immortal, deathless, tearless bodies, and then that great company will rise into the air in a great cloud to be met in the sky by the Lord Jesus Christ Himself. This is the order wherever the Rapture is mentioned. In I Corinthians 15 we see this order:

> For the trumpet shall sound, and the dead shall be raised incorruptible, and we shall be changed.

The same order we saw in I Thessalonians 4:

> The dead in Christ shall rise first: then we which are alive and remain shall be caught up together with them in the clouds, to meet the Lord in the air.

In John 11 we read that Jesus told Martha the same thing. Lazarus died and the two sisters, Mary and Martha, were in great sorrow. Finally the Lord came and was met first by Martha and then by Mary. When Martha met the Lord she said, "Lord, if thou hadst been here, my brother had not died." The Lord assured her that Lazarus would live again. Martha believed in the resurrection of the dead, but knew nothing of the blessed hope of the resurrection of the dead at the coming of the Lord in the Rapture, and so she answered this assurance of the Lord with the words found in John 11:24:

> I know that he shall rise again in the resurrection at the last day.

She knew only of a general resurrection at the last day, an error which is still believed by countless numbers of Christians, but Jesus had better news for her. He told her that the believers would not have to wait until the resurrection of the last day. That resurrection is only for the unsaved, but at least a thousand years before that, at the coming again of the Lord, the saved will all be raised and caught up to meet the Lord, for the answer of Jesus anticipates the revelation of the mystery of the Rapture as later given by Paul in Thessalonians and in Corinthians. Notice, therefore, the answer of the Lord to Martha. Here it is:

> I am the resurrection, and the life; he that believeth in me, though he were dead, yet shall he live; and whosoever liveth and believeth in me shall never die (John 11:25, 26).

Now notice that this is the resurrection of believers. He says not a word of the resurrection of unbelievers. Their resurrection has nothing to do with the event Jesus refers to in this passage. He says:

> He that believeth in me, though he were dead, yet shall he live: and whosoever liveth and believeth in me shall never die.

In other words, when Jesus comes again, His return will affect only the believers, both the dead and the living, but the order will be the same as everywhere else. First the dead in Christ ("he that believeth in me, though he were dead") and then they that remain ("whosoever liveth and believeth in me"). How carefully God guards the harmony of Scripture!

I CORINTHIANS 15:51

Soon the day will come when the last believer will be added to the body of Christ before His return and then Jesus will come from heaven to take us out of this wicked world, and for us it will be the day when "death is swallowed up in victory." This is the hope of the Christian: not to make the world a better place to live in, but to prepare to leave this world before God comes to punish it for its rejection of Christ. The Christian looks ahead and all is bright. If he dies tomorrow he will be with the Lord. If he lives till Jesus comes, he will be caught away before the storm of judgment breaks. How wonderful! No wonder, then, that Paul could close this passage with the shout, "O death, where is thy sting? O grave, where is thy victory?" Then he gives the reason: "The sting of death is sin; and the strength of sin is the law. But thanks be unto God, which giveth us the victory through our Lord Jesus Christ." Two things can alarm us: the law and death, but the law cannot touch the believer because its penalty has been paid, and death cannot harm us because the sting of death is gone, and that sting is sin. We do not fear to meet God in death, but we fear to meet God in sin, and if that sin is removed, death has lost its sting, for the sting of death is sin.

THE STING OF DEATH

Bees have only one stinger, and this is so constructed that when a bee stings it always leaves the stinger in the victim, and after that it is a stingless bee. The same bee can never sting twice or sting two victims. A few years ago a bee stung my oldest son above the eye, as with a scream of pain he brushed the bee away and fell crying in the grass. Immediately the same bee flew at my younger son's head and with a louder scream he fell into the grass, crying to me for help while the bee circled about his head. I raised him up against his will with this remark: "That bee is harmless; it cannot sting you." He was frightened and said, "But look at him and hear him buzz at me." Then I took him to his older brother and said, "See that sting in your brother's eyebrow? That is the bee's stinger. He left it in your elder brother and now the bee can buzz, but it cannot sting. It has only one sting and that one was left in Richard." I removed the sting and quoted the verse, "The sting of death is sin." Yes, that is it. Only sin can make us fear death, and without sin death cannot harm us. It can only usher us into God's blessed presence. It may frighten us, but it cannot hurt us because the sting is gone. The sting of death is sin, but my Elder Brother took my sin and bore my sin in His own body on the tree, and death cannot sting that body twice. I am in that body by faith and my head has borne the sting, and now death cannot harm me. My Elder Brother took away the sting of death, even sin, and now death may alarm us by its doleful buzzing, but, praise God, it cannot hurt us, and now we can live without worry if we will only trust Him. We can say, "Whether we live, or . . . die, we are the Lord's." "Thanks be to God, which giveth us the victory through our Lord Jesus Christ" who took the sting of death.

> I know not when my Lord may come,
> At night or noonday fair,
> Nor if I'll walk the vale with Him,
> Or "meet Him in the air."
> But "I know whom I have believed,
> And am persuaded that He is able
> To keep that which I've committed
> Unto Him against that day."

This is a great mystery, but I speak concerning Christ and the Church.

V

> . . . I am made a minister, according to the dispensation of God which is given to me for you, to fulfil the word of God; even the mystery which hath been hid from ages and from generations, but now is made manifest to his saints: to whom God would make known what is the riches of the glory of this mystery among the Gentiles; which is Christ in you, the hope of glory (Colossians 1:25-27).

We have considered the mystery of Israel's rejection and the setting aside of the kingdom, while God through the Holy Spirit was calling out the mystery of the body of Christ to be His bride, and the mystery of the Rapture, when this Church, the body of Christ, will be taken up to meet her Lord in the air. Some of the other mysteries have already been expounded, such as the mystery of the Incarnation of Christ. Here is a mystery which is the basis and foundation for all. It is the mystery of regeneration. Paul calls it the mystery of "Christ in you, the hope of glory." Until you have experienced that mysterious transformation which we call the new birth and regeneration you cannot understand any of the other mysteries of the Scriptures. The word "mystery" in Scripture, you will remember, comes from the Greek root word *muo* which means "a secret." Only members of the true Church of Christ, which is His body, can know the secrets of the Word of God. It is for this reason that thousands of Bible students who know the Bible from cover to cover from a literary and critical standpoint never see the mysteries of the Word, while some other illiterate and uneducated believer sees more in this precious Book in five minutes than the most learned unregenerate professor of theology sees in a lifetime. There are learned Bible scholars and teachers who never see the truth of the virgin birth or the truth of the deity of Christ or the necessity of the blood, the bodily resurrection of Christ and His second coming. It seems strange that with an open Bible before them they do not see these truths which to us are perfectly clear. But, after all, it is not strange, for these things are mysteries known only to those who know the spiritual code and have been initiated into the fraternity of God's family by the mystery of the new birth. Jesus said that these things were hidden from the wise and the prudent and that they were revealed to babes. A babe is one that is born, and so, until you are born again into the family of God you cannot receive these things in your heart.

> But the natural man receiveth not the things of the Spirit of God; for they are foolishness unto him: neither can he

know them, because they are spiritually discerned (I Corinthians 2:14).

There is your answer to this question: Why do not all who read the Bible see these marvelous truths of revelation? Jesus said, "Verily, verily I say unto thee, Except a man be born again, he cannot see the kingdom of God." The first requirement, therefore, to understand the Scriptures is to be born again. This new birth is called by Paul a mystery, "Christ in you, the hope of glory." Jesus also emphasizes the mysterious character of the process by which a sinner becomes a saint, and a child of the devil becomes a child of God. Psychology may explain many things, but it has never been able to fathom the psychology of regeneration. It is beyond the realm of all philosophy and psychology. It is in the realm of the supernatural; and human psychology and philosophy generally deny the element of the supernatural, but Jesus assures us that the new birth cannot be understood except by the Spirit. He says in John 3:

> That which is born of the flesh is flesh; and that which is born of the Spirit is spirit. Marvel not that I said unto thee, Ye must be born again. The wind bloweth where it listeth, and thou hearest the sound thereof, but canst not tell whence it cometh, and whither it goeth; so is every one that is born of the spirit (John 3:6-8).

It is a deep mystery. One wonders how by a simple act of faith in the Lord Jesus Christ a man is changed from a vile, cursing, drunken blasphemer into a praying, hymn-singing saint, but it happens. I have seen it many times and have experienced the revolutionary power and transforming dynamite of the Gospel in my own life. By an act of faith, the thief becomes an honest, respectable citizen; the harlot is made pure; the liar is made truthful; the drunkard is sobered for good; and the sinner is made a saint.

WHAT IS THE NEW BIRTH?

Sad to say, the real meaning of the new birth is greatly misunderstood by many professing Christians. This is partly due to a translation of the third chapter of John which gives the wrong impression. The words "born again" are really incorrect. A man is not born "over again" in the sense that God does anything at all to the nature of the sinner. The old Adam remains the same. The old nature of the sinner is left undisturbed. By our first birth we are so corrupt and incorrigibly wicked that God looks at us and says, "There is no use trying to do anything with that. It is hopeless. Even My own omnipotence cannot make the fallen nature of Adam better." Instead, the Lord ignores the old nature of sin and sets about to make an "entirely new creation." Paul tells us in II Corinthians 5:17:

> Therefore if any man be in Christ, he is a new creature: old things are passed away; behold, all things are become new.

The saved man is not a sinner "made over." It is not a regeneration of the old man. Instead, it is a new thing, a new nature which God implants in the believer alongside of the old which is still there. Spurgeon once said, "Every new man is two men — the old and the new," and so the believer has within him immediately after he is saved two natures: the nature of sinful, fallen Adam which can never do good and the new nature of God which cannot sin. Of the old nature God says that it is "deceitful above all things, and desperately wicked." Paul, recognizing this thirty years after he was saved, confessed, "I know that in me (that is, in my flesh), dwelleth no good thing." But the new nature is holy and sinless because it is the life of God imparted and "Christ in you, the hope of glory." Peter says in his second epistle that we "are partakers of the divine nature." We possess the life of God as well as the death of Adam. God dwells in us. We are temples of the Holy Ghost, and Christ is in us "the hope of glory."

Jesus said to Nicodemus, "Verily, verily, I say unto thee, Except a man be *born again*, he cannot see the kingdom of God." The word translated "again" in this passage is *anothen* in the Greek, and by referring to your concordance or your Greek lexicon you will notice that the word *anothen* should have been translated "from above" and the verse should read, "Verily, verily, I say unto thee, Except a man be born *from above*, he cannot see the kingdom of God." It is a spiritual birth, not a natural rebirth. Jesus said, "So is every one that is born of the Spirit."

THE MYSTERY

That, my friend, is the mystery of the new birth, for two natures dwell in the believer: one nature which is not subject to the law of God, neither indeed can be, and another nature which seeks always to do the will of God. The one nature is called the flesh, and the other is called the spirit, because one is born of the flesh and the other of the Spirit. Of these two Paul says:

> For the flesh lusteth against the Spirit, and the Spirit against the flesh: and these are contrary the one to the other: so that YE cannot do the things that ye would. But if ye be led of the Spirit, ye are not under the law (Galatians 5:17-18).

In Romans 7 Paul says:

> For that which I do I allow not: for what I would, that do I not; but what I hate, that I do. If then I do that which I would not, I consent unto the law that it is good. Now then it is no more I that do it, but sin that dwelleth in me. For I know that in me (that is, in my flesh,) dwelleth no good thing: for to will is present with me; but how to perform that which is good I find not . . . I find then a law, that, when I would do good, evil is present with me. For I delight in the law of God after the inward man [the new man]: but I see another law in my members, warring against the law of my mind, and bringing me into captivity to the law of sin [the old man] which is in my members. O wretched man that I am! who shall deliver me from the body of this death? (Romans 7:15-24).

Before considering the answer to Paul's question, "Who shall deliver me from the body of this death?" and there is deliverance, thank God, as we shall see — I want you to see the teaching of this passage. Paul recognizes the fact that the flesh is still there and that there is a battle on in his life between the Old and the New. Happy is the man who recognizes this fact, for only as you are aware of the presence of the enemy can you successfully cope with him. To close your eyes and say, "He is gone," will not do. No, we are to face the facts, and only then can we have Scriptural and real victory. How we need this lesson! My friend, are you troubled because you have a difficult struggle with your old nature? Are you discouraged because you try hard to do what you know is God's will and find a battle of temptation and trial? That very fact should encourage you, for it is the evidence that you want to please God and fight against the old man. The evidence of the new life is not a peaceful complacency without a battle, but the consciousness of a struggle and the realization that alone we are defeated and that God alone can give us absolute victory over the flesh.

THE OLD AND THE NEW

In I John we have two passages which have confused many of God's dear people. The first is in I John 1:8-10:

> If we say that we have no sin, we deceive ourselves, and the truth is not in us. If we confess our sins, he is faithful and just to forgive us our sins, and to cleanse us from all unrighteousness. If we say that we have not sinned, we make him a liar, and his word is not in us.

These are solemn words, spoken to believers, but in I John 3:9 we read:

> Whosoever is born of God doth not commit sin; for his seed remaineth in him: and he cannot sin, because he is born of God.

Both passages are from the Word of God and both are true, but unless you recognize the presence of both natures in the believer you will be helplessly confused. You will have to reject one or the other, but when you remember that the Holy Spirit in I John 1:8 and 10 is speaking of the old nature, which is incorrigibly sinful, and in I John 3:9 He is speaking of that which is born "of God," everything is clear. The first reference is to your nature by your first birth; the other refers to the nature of your second birth, and then both passages are true. The old is always prone to sin and the new cannot sin because it is born of God.

True Scriptural victory can never be had if we fail to recognize the true nature of the old Adam.

THE VICTORY

But someone asks, "Do we have to suffer defeat at the hands of that old nature, the flesh, all our lives?" Absolutely not. That is the very point of recognizing the two natures. The new is of God, born of the Spirit, and, therefore, has the potentialities of omnipotence. The old is very strong because it is dead, and strangely enough, the longer that corpse lies around, the stronger it becomes. But in the new nature we have the potentialities of daily victory over the old. After Paul has complained of the struggle and cries out, "O wretched man that I am! who shall deliver me from the body of this death?" he immediately gives the answer: "I thank God through Jesus Christ our Lord." "There is therefore now no condemnation to them which are in Christ Jesus, who walk not after the flesh, but after the Spirit." Yes, there is victory — not in our own strength, but in Christ. He is in us, the hope of glory, and the victory comes when we recognize the fact that in our own strength we are defeated, and yield the battle into His hands. Jesus said, "Without me ye can do nothing," but Paul could say and I can say, "I can do all things through Christ which strengtheneth me."

VICTORY BY SURRENDER

The only way to have victory is by surrender. That sounds like a paradox, but it is true. In Philippians 3:3 we read,

> For we are the circumcision, which worship God in the spirit, and rejoice in Christ Jesus, and have no confidence in the flesh.

Here is the secret if you are defeated by the flesh and habit and the lusts of the old nature. Think of what you are in Christ. Rejoice in the fact that your salvation does not depend on your victory, but the victory He gained for you. Recognize the fact that you cannot cope with your flesh, and then yield completely to Him. Surrender to Him. Have you tried to overcome that thing in your life which is defeating you? Have you struggled and resolved and failed? Then listen. Kneel before Him and confess that you have failed, tell Him you are weary of trying and that you know that you cannot conquer that thing and let Him fight the battle for you. There is victory through surrender. There is strength through yielding. There is a sane philosophy in the statement of the old colored fellow who was known to live a life of holiness and victory. Someone asked him, "Joe, how come you are never defeated and you never seem to fall before temptation?" The old fellow replied, "Whenever the debil done rap at mah door, I just say to Jesus, 'There am that debil again and ah caint beat him. You just go to the door fo me, Jesus.' And when the debil done heah dat, he run right away." Yes, let Jesus win the battle for you. To be sure, there is a battle, and will be till you meet Him but —

Thanks be to God, which giveth us the victory through our Lord Jesus Christ.

CHAPTER FIVE

The Antichrist

I. THE PERSONAL ANTICHRIST

The most horrible and sinister picture given in the Scriptures is the picture of the Antichrist, called also the Man of Sin, the Son of Perdition and that Wicked One. At the time of the end, in the Day of the Lord, he will be revealed to set up his wicked reign. Unrestrained by that which now restrains him, he will have free reign to put into action all his hellish and fiendish powers. After the Church is caught away and He that now hindereth is removed, "then shall that Wicked one be revealed . . . whose coming is after the working of Satan" (II Thess. 2:8, 9). The picture of this terrible individual is found throughout the Word of God. The slimy trail of the serpent can be traced from the first book of the Bible to the last. The first mention that we have of the Antichrist is in the Protevangelium in Genesis 3:15. Here we are told that God will set enmity between the seed of the woman and the seed of the serpent. As the seed of the woman was a person, even the Christ, so, too, the seed of the serpent will be a person, even the Antichrist. We will trace the trail of the Wicked One, from this point in Genesis 3:15, until he becomes the personal Antichrist of the end-time.

We might select a dozen or more extensive passages from the Word as a basis for our discourse on the Antichrist, and we shall refer to these several passages later on, but wish to take as our point of departure the second letter of Paul to the Thessalonians. Here we are given a very complete and clear picture of the Man of Sin, the False Prophet of Revelation; and even without reference to the rest of the passages in Scripture we can from this one book gain considerable information about this Man of Sin.

The two epistles of Paul to the Thessalonians were written to correct certain serious errors that had crept into the Thessalonian Church. In both instances they were errors concerning the second coming of the Lord Jesus. It is a fact that more errors creep into circles that hold the second coming of the Lord than any others. This is just what might be expected. It is true today that the Fundamentalist groups are the most shaken by errors. The explanation, however, is not hard to find. Wherever the second coming of Christ is taught and preached, there is power. There is warmth and activity, and there souls are saved. The devil knows this and for that reason he does not leave the lovers of the Lord's return alone. He concentrates on them and summons his cohorts especially for an attack upon all those who teach and preach this blessed truth. Those who minimize the doctrine of the last things are free from the attacks of Satan, for he knows the wisdom of "letting well enough alone." He will not awaken them from their deadness and lethargy. But let the second coming be preached, and immediately there is work for him to do. The devil has far too much sense to waste his ammunition on his friends. The devil knows enough not to shoot at dead birds. Hence those groups that are the most active for the cause of Christ are the favorite targets of the Evil One, and this accounts for the rather frequent stumbling of the Fundamentalists.

We need not be alarmed at this today for it was also true in the Thessalonian Church as early as the days of Paul. Both times Paul wrote to them they had been taught a false doctrine by those whom the devil could use as his tools to pervert the truth of the Lord's return. In the first letter of Paul the error had to do with the Rapture. Paul had taught the Christians at Thessalonica that the Lord was soon coming to set up His kingdom and that they all would have a share in it. This had made them happy, but then something happened that disturbed them very much. Some of their number had died. These poor Thessalonians were heartbroken. They thought that now these who had fallen asleep would have no part in Christ's return and kingdom, as they supposed that these would not be resurrected until *after* the return and the kingdom. So Paul writes to correct this error. He tells them not to worry about those who sleep in Jesus as they will have a share in the glory. But let us allow Paul to speak for himself in the passage from I Thessalonians 4:

> But I would not have you to be ignorant, brethren, concerning them which are asleep, that ye sorrow not, even as others which have no hope.
> For if ["ei" in the Greek, meaning "since"] we believe that Jesus died and rose again, even so them also which sleep in Jesus will God bring with him [will God through Jesus bring].
> For this we say unto you by the word of the Lord, that we which are alive and remain unto the coming of the Lord will in no wise prevent [precede] them which are asleep.
> For the Lord himself shall descend from heaven with a shout, with the voice of the archangel, and with the trump of God: and the dead in Christ shall rise first: then we which are alive and remain shall be caught up together with them in the clouds, to meet the Lord in the air: and so shall we ever be with the Lord.
> Wherefore comfort one another with these words (I Thess. 4:13-18).

Paul assures them that when Christ comes for His saints, the Rapture will include the dead in Christ as well, and that they will even precede the living ones. Surely this passage from I Thessalonians is self-explanatory.

After this error was corrected, another soon crept in. This time the error had to do with the Day of the Lord, which Scripture declares is that terrible time between the Rapture (the coming of Christ *for* His saints) and the second coming (the coming of the Lord *with* His saints). Someone had been teaching these Thessalonians that the Rapture was a thing of the past and that the Day of the

Lord was already present. We can imagine the alarm of
these Christians at this thought. Paul had taught that at
the Rapture they would be caught up with the resurrected
saints (I Thess. 4:13-18). Now they were told that the
persecution which they were experiencing was the Day of
the Lord (the Great Tribulation). This could mean only
one thing, namely, that the Rapture was past and that
they had been left behind. Surely it is no wonder that
they were in consternation. This error Paul seeks to correct in the Second Epistle to the Thessalonians:

> Now we beseech you, brethren, by the coming of our
> Lord Jesus Christ, and by our gathering together unto him,
> that ye be not soon shaken in mind, or be troubled, neither
> by spirit, nor by word, nor by letter as from us, as that the
> day of Christ is at hand (II Thess. 2:1-2).

Notice that Paul begins by beseeching them by the
coming of the Lord and their gathering together. It is
very important for a proper understanding of the Tribulation that we have the distinction well in mind between
the coming of the Lord and our gathering together unto
Him, His coming *for* His saints and His coming *with* His
saints. One is before the Tribulation and the other is immediately after the Tribulation. Since the Thessalonians
were confused about the Tribulation (Day of the Lord),
Paul first of all wants to make clear the distinctions between His coming and our gathering. The Tribulation is
the period of time between the two.

It is very unfortunate that the second verse is a poor
translation of the Greek. Instead of "day of Christ" we
should read "day of the Lord," and instead of "at hand"
we should read "present." The word in the Greek which
is translated Christ is *kurios* (Lord) and not *Christos*
(Christ). So, too, with the words "at hand." The same
word which is here translated "at hand" is translated in
Romans 8:38, I Corinthians 3:22, Galatians 1:4 and
Hebrews 9:9 as "present." The correct reading is this:
"That ye be not soon shaken in mind as by spirit or by

word or by letter as from us as that the day of the Lord is present."

"No, no," says Paul, "the Day of the Lord is not yet present; neither is the Rapture past."

> Let no man deceive you by any means: for that day shall not come, except there come a falling away first, and that man of sin be revealed, the son of perdition; who opposeth and exalteth himself above all that is called God, or that is worshipped; so that he as God sitteth in the temple of God, shewing himself that he is God.
>
> Remember ye not, that, when I was yet with you, I told you these things? (II Thess. 2:3, 4, 5).

The Day of the Lord cannot come till the Man of Sin be revealed. He it is who will be the main actor and it will be by his satanic influence that the terrible Day of Jehovah with its tribulations shall be ushered in.

> And now ye know what withholdeth that he might be revealed in his time.
>
> For the mystery of iniquity doth already work; only he who now letteth [hindereth. "Let" is an old English word for "hinder"] will let, until he be taken out of the way.
>
> And then shall that Wicked be revealed . . . (II Thess. 2:6, 7, 8).

There is One who now hinders and withholds the revelation of the Man of Sin. That One is the Spirit of God and at the Rapture, when He is taken out of the way and with the Church, upon whom He came at Pentecost, rises to meet the Lord in the air — then and then only will the Antichrist be free to put his age-old schemes of the devil into operation. The spirit of the Antichrist is held in check now, while the Spirit is gathering out the bride. The moment the bride is complete and Christ has gathered out of the Gentiles a people for His Name, then the hindrance will be removed, the personal Antichrist will be revealed and the Day of the Lord will be ushered in.

THE ANTICHRIST IS A MYSTERIOUS CHARACTER

The spirit of the Antichrist is called the mystery of iniquity. Surely there is much mystery concerning Him and yet so much is revealed in the Word that we have ample material, without delving into those things which are too mysterious. The full light upon Antichrist will come after the catching away of the bride, and thank God, we will not be here. Ours will be a bird's-eye view. One thing seems certain from the many references to him: he will be a counterfeit and a clever imitation of the true Christ. His aim will be to so closely imitate and simulate Christ that if it were possible the very elect of God would be deceived. If you will bear in mind this outstanding characteristic, it will clarify many of the passages that refer to him. Since the devil heard the announcement of "enmity between . . . thy seed and her seed," it has been his ruse to conceal the distinction between "thy seed and her seed."

II. THE SPIRIT OF THE ANTICHRIST

In considering the identification of the Antichrist we shall first consider the spirit of the Antichrist and then the person of the Antichrist. There can be no doubt but that the spirit of the Antichrist is the spirit of the Evil One. He is Satan, that old serpent, the devil. The person of the Antichrist will be an individual, energized by the devil himself. His great fight is between himself and the seed of the woman (Christ), hence his imitation of Him. We may trace the struggle from Genesis to Revelation. When the Lord said unto the serpent that the seed of the woman should "bruise his head," he determined right there and then that his only hope was either to prevent the birth of the seed of the woman or to destroy Him after He came. The easier way, of course, would be to intercept the seed and prevent His birth. Throughout the whole Old Testament therefore we see his cunning devices to destroy and corrupt the line of the seed. It began soon after the fall. There we see the policy of the devil in a nutshell.

SATAN THOUGHT ABEL WAS THE SEED

When the first two children were born of our first parents, we may rest assured that Satan scrutinized them very carefully to determine which, if any, was the promised seed. He soon saw that Abel was a child of faith. He saw that his offering was accepted and Cain's was rejected. *There is the seed or at least the line of the seed,* thought the devil and he conspired to have him put to death before he could bring forth seed. He succeeded in using Cain to put his brother to death. That it was through Satan, that Cain did it, is plain from the New Testament statement that Cain was of that wicked one (I John 3:12). But God overruled the attack of Satan. He had been too hasty and misjudged the case. God raised up Seth as the next link in the line of the seed. Satan's next attack therefore was upon the line of Seth.

> And it came to pass, when men began to multiply on the face of the earth, and daughters were born unto them, that the sons of God saw the daughters of men that they were fair; and they took them wives of all which they chose . . .
> There were giants in the earth in those days; and also after that, when the sons of God came in unto the daughters of men, and they bare children to them, the same became mighty men which were of old, men of renown (Gen. 6:1, 2, 4).

This was Satan's next step in his attempt to corrupt the seed. He had failed to kill and stop the line of the seed; he now tried to corrupt it. And so we have the unholy union of demons and women and from this freakish union were born certain monstrous beings called giants (Anakim). They were men of great power because they were half man and half devil. But God saw the devil's motive and He preserved one line that remained uncorrupted. While every imagination of man's heart was to do evil continually, there was one man who found grace in the eyes of the Lord. This man was Noah, and it was through this man that the line of the seed was to be perpetuated. Accordingly the Lord sent the Flood to destroy the freakish results of Satan's attempt to foil God's plan but spared Noah and his family, because through him ran the line of the seed.

For a long time after the Flood, the devil seemed to be

confused. He could not find the line in which the seed was being preserved. Wickedness increased apace and the knowledge of the Lord seemed to fail from the earth. But again God raised up one man and came to him to make His promise of the seed to him. This man was Abraham. You may rest assured that Satan overheard the promise of the seed to Abraham and we can imagine him exclaiming, "Ah, that is what I have been looking for!" He knew immediately, that the line was to be through Abraham and immediately, he set out to stop the coming of the seed. Before this, he had tried to corrupt the seed through the unholy union of demons and humans. This time he attempted it in a different way.

But Sarai was barren; she had no child (Gen. 11:30).

How significant these words! For a long time, from the Flood to Abraham, the devil had been unable to trace the line of the seed, but as soon as God spoke to Abraham, he was on the trail again and we read: *But Sarai was barren*. But God again intervened and Sarai conceived in her old age and bore Isaac. Isaac now became the target of the Wicked One.

And Isaac entreated the Lord for his wife, because she was barren (Gen. 25:21).

Again God intervened and overruled, and the seed was perpetuated in Jacob.

So we might trace the line. Suffice it to call attention to the children of Israel in Egypt. See Satan's attempt there to destroy the whole seed.

However, in spite of all of Satan's efforts, the seed did come. For a long time Satan did not discover the line through which the seed was to come. One thing he knew: it would be of the seed of Judah and through David. He knew that the seed would be born in Bethlehem, for you may rest assured that Satan knows the Bible. And so when he saw the shepherds going to Bethlehem, he followed, and as soon as he was assured that the babe in the

manger was the seed, he began his plotting to destroy
not the line of the seed, but the seed itself. He instigated
Herod to have all the children in Bethlehem under two
years put to death. But the Lord had snatched the seed
out of his reach and caused His parents to take Him to
Egypt. Foiled again, Satan would not give up. No sooner
had Jesus entered upon His ministry than he attempted
the fall of the seed in the temptation in the wilderness.
Again he failed.

From this time we see the devil in a never-ceasing
attempt to kill the seed. He sought to use the scribes,
the Pharisees and the Sadducees, but all to no avail, for
His time was not yet. Finally, after three and a half
years, he saw the possibility of success. The time of popu-
lar favor was past and he saw the seed being rejected of
the people. He thought the time to strike had come. Satan
entered Judas. He was preparing for the master stroke —
the personal Antichrist. The entering of Satan into Judas
was Satan's first attempt to set up the personal Antichrist
in his ill-timed attempt to destroy the seed, and it seemed
that the plan was successful, for he saw the seed led into
the judgment hall and there condemned. As soon as he
saw the result he had no more use for Judas and uncere-
moniously destroyed him. Thus does Satan with all that
serve him. At the end he casts them into perdition.

Imagine the rejoicing among the armies of the devil as
they see the seed condemned to die, led out to Calvary's
Cross to be put to death in the most shameful way known.
While the mad mob howled at the foot of the Cross and
the host of heaven gasped at the spectacle of their Creator
upon the Cross, wild pandemonium broke out among the
legions of the pit. Apparently the struggle between the
seed of the woman and the seed of the serpent had proved
successful for the latter. "It was a long and bitter struggle," chuckled old Satan, "but at last I have succeeded."
I can imagine him chuckling. "There He is and I am

king." But there was a surprise in store for him. He had
been apparently successful before, and God had done the
surprising thing. So, too, here. After three days and
three nights the seed arose from the dead, triumphant
over death and hell and Satan. Now what will Satan do?
All his scheming of centuries and millenniums has been
put to naught and he is compelled to start all over again.
The seed is taken into heaven and now he levels all his
attacks upon those that are of the mother of that seed and
the children of that seed. When his time shall come he
will make one more bold attempt, when for the second
time Satan enters Judas and attempts to foil the plan of
the seed. This will be through the personal Antichrist
of the end-time.

III. THE PERSON OF THE ANTICHRIST

Having considered the spirit of the Antichrist (Satan
himself) and his many attempts to overcome the Christ,
we come now to the study of the personal Antichrist of
the end-time. There have been many, many guesses concerning this person. Ideas and opinions have not been
lacking. In the days of the early Church the consensus
was that Nero was the Antichrist, and, to be sure, he looked
very much like him. However, if the early Christians had
remembered that the Antichrist would not be revealed
until after the Rapture they would not have supposed
Nero to have been the Antichrist. During the times of the
Reformation the Pope was considered the Antichrist and
the Pope in turn characterized the Reformers as the Antichrist. Today there are many who suppose that Mussolini
of Italy is the Antichrist. Others are very positive it is
Hitler. Let us remember: "That day shall not come until
he that hindereth be taken out of the way. And then shall
that Wicked be revealed."

INCARNATION OF JUDAS ISCARIOT

That Judas Iscariot, the betrayer of Jesus, was the
devil's first attempt to produce the personal Antichrist is

soundly supported by Scripture. That the devil's second attempt to overthrow the work of Christ is through this same person will appear from the following Scripture passages. Satan entered into Judas once, and when he comes as the Antichrist of the end-time, it will be as an incarnation of the betrayer of the seed, viz., Judas Iscariot. The evidence is convincing, when we consider several of the passages that deal with this matter.

> While I was with them in the world, I kept them in thy name: those that thou gavest me I have kept, and none of them is lost, but the son of perdition; that the scripture might be fulfilled (John 17:12).
> Let no man deceive you by any means: for that day shall not come, except there come a falling away first, and that man of sin be revealed, the son of perdition (II Thess. 2:3).

Notice here that we have quoted the only two passages in the Word of God where the name "Son of Perdition" is used. In one instance it is applied to Judas Iscariot and in the second it is applied to the Man of Sin, the Antichrist. Surely here is a close association. They are the same. They are called the same.

> Then entered Satan into Judas surnamed Iscariot, being of the number of the twelve (Luke 22:3).

This is the only passage which says that Satan entered into a man. We have many, many examples of demons taking their abode in men and women, but here we read that Satan personally, as the Prince of Devils, made his temporary abode in Judas. But the argument is made still more conclusive by the statement in the Gospel according to John:

> Jesus answered them, Have not I chosen you twelve, and one of you is a devil? (John 6:70).

Judas is called *devil* — not *a devil*. In the original it is: "One of you is devil [*Diabolis*]. Diabolis is the devil and Satan. He does not say that Judas is a demon, but devil. In Acts 1:25 we are told that Judas "might go to his own place." In the light of who he was we can understand that it was the devil's own place (the place prepared for the devil and his angels).

Judas, then, will be the Antichrist. The spirit of the Antichrist (when the Spirit of God, which now hindereth, will be taken away) will enter once more into mankind and cause to be born another freak half man and half devil who will be the incarnation of the devil. When you remember that the Antichrist will attempt to simulate the true Christ in every detail, you see more and more the subtlety of Satan in this procedure. Some of you may object; you may not believe that Satan can cause a supernatural conception, but Scripture plainly teaches it. The sixth chapter of Genesis tells of the sons of God and the daughters of men — the parents of those freaks, the giants. Job 1 identifies the devil as one of the sons of God. In Jude we have the clearest statement of all:

And the angels which kept not their first estate, but left their own habitation, he hath reserved in everlasting chains under darkness unto the judgment of that great day.

Even as Sodom and Gomorrha, and the cities about them in like manner, giving themselves over to fornication, and going after strange flesh . . . (Jude 6, 7).

That it is possible, therefore, is clearly taught by what Scripture says of what Satan had done in the past. Moreover the devil has power to give life (by permission). He is said to give life to the image of the beast (Rev. 13) and is said in II Thessalonians 2 to come with all deceivableness and lying wonders. He performed miracles in the past and he will be the great miracle-worker in the time of the Great Tribulation.

CLEARS UP MYSTERY OF JUDAS

If Judas was Satan incarnate, we can understand the mystery of the remorse of Judas and his repentance. He repented. He was filled with remorse, yet he found no forgiveness. If Judas were a man like others, how can we ever account for the fact that though he had remorse and sorrow, God did not hear him? He was Satan, and there is no salvation for Satan. Judas was sent into the world to be the betrayer, that the Scriptures might be fulfilled. If this be true, then Judas "never had a chance."

To be sure, he did not. Yet God says it is not His will
that any should perish, but that *all* should come to repentance. If Judas, therefore, were a man like others, he
would be an exception, and there can be no exceptions to
all. Since he was and will be Satan incarnate, the mystery
is solved, for Satan fell beyond hope of restoration. Thus
he went to his own place. He had a special place. We
have here a suggestion that he is kept there until the time
for the last attempt of Satan shall come.

In Genesis 3:15 we have this prediction, for Christ is
called the seed of the woman. The Antichrist is seen there
as the seed of the serpent. In both cases an incarnation
occurs: an incarnation of God and, on the other hand, a
clever imitation, an incarnation of Satan.

IV. HIS POLICY AND CLAIMS

In considering the policy and claims of the personal
Antichrist, we must remind you again of a key that will
help much in understanding his methods. Remember that
he is the *Anti*christ. As we trace his course through the
Word, we find that, like the saints in revelation, he follows "the Lamb whithersoever he goeth." His purpose is
to make men believe that he is true Christ and God, and
therefore he imitates Christ, making the same claims and
doing many of the same miracles. For this reason both
Jew and Gentile will readily accept Him as the great
master mind and coming deliverer.

His rise will be sudden. This is also in imitation of
Christ. Our Lord for thirty years remained in obscurity
in His home in Nazareth, and the silence of those years is
broken only once in Luke 2. Then, when His time had
come, He was baptized in the Jordan, and after the temptation in the wilderness He at once revealed Himself in
the miracle of the making of water into wine at Cana of
Galilee, and many disciples believed on Him because of
the miracle. So, too, the Antichrist will remain in obscurity, till "he be taken out of the way" and then shall

that Wicked be "revealed." He may even now be in the world. He may be preparing for his hellish work. Then, when his time comes and the restraint and hindrance of the Holy Spirit are removed, he shall suddenly appear. He will come with the baptism of hell and announce himself by miracles and lying wonders. His active reign will be for a time and times and a half a time, or approximately three and a half years (the length of Jesus' active ministry here).

Jesus said, "I am the light of the world." He, too, will come, acclaiming himself as the light. But instead it will be darkness.

> Even him, whose coming is after the working of Satan with all power and signs and lying wonders.
> And with all deceivableness of unrighteousness in them that perish; because they received not the love of the truth, that they might be saved.
> And for this cause God shall send them strong delusion, that they should believe a lie (II Thess. 2:9, 10, 11).

Undoubtedly one of the elements of his marvelous success in gaining the hearts of the people lies in the fact that he will come promising the very thing that is uppermost in the hearts of many men today: peace. The world is sick of war and is looking for peace. Jesus is the Prince of Peace and, when He comes again, He will come as the Prince of Peace. The devil knows this and will try to defeat the Prince of Peace by offering peace before Jesus comes and thus steal the hearts of men, only that he may set the stage for the most terrible slaughter the world has known.

> And I saw when the Lamb opened one of the seals, and I heard, as it were the noise of thunder, and one of the beasts saying, Come and see.
> And I saw, and behold a white horse: and he that sat on him had a bow; and a crown was given unto him: and he went forth conquering and to conquer (Rev. 6:1, 2).

Here is the white horse of peace, upon which the Wicked One ushers in that short period of time of the Tribulation. When the Antichrist comes, he will come with the promise of peace on earth.

> And in his estate shall stand up a vile person, to whom
> they shall not give the honour of the kingdom: but he shall
> come in peaceably, and obtain the kingdom by flatteries . . .
> And after the league made with him he shall work deceit-
> fully: for he shall come up, and shall become strong with a
> small people.
> He shall enter peaceably even upon the fattest places of
> the province . . . (Dan. 11:21, 23, 24a).

His first move is to gain the confidence of the people,
and especially the Jews. He needs the Jewish wealth to
carry on his program, and his first attempt is to gain the
favor of the Jews. He will aid them in the return to the
land and, in general, will show them favors.

> He shall scatter among them the prey, and spoil, and
> riches: yea, and he shall forecast his devices against the
> strong holds, even for a time.
> And he shall stir up his power and his courage against
> the king of the south with a great army; and the king of
> the south shall be stirred up to battle with a very great and
> mighty army; but he shall not stand: for they shall forecast
> devices against him (Daniel 11:24b-25).

Here we have the clever ruse of the devil. He will take
up for the Jews their cause against their old enemy the
Ishmaelites (the king of the south). The trouble is even
now brewing between the old enemies, Isaac's children
and Ishmael's children. Recently the Mohammedan
powers caused the massacre of hundreds of Jews in
Palestine. This is but the beginning of sorrow. When the
Antichrist shall come his master stroke will be to guarantee peace to the Jews by offering to subdue the Mohammedan menace. But this peace will be but for a short
time, only long enough for him to gain his point and his
influence, and then he will turn upon those he has pledged
to protect with all the fiendish and hellish hatred that
Satan himself is able to muster.

> Then shall he return into his land with great riches; and
> his heart shall be against the holy covenant; and he shall
> do exploits, and return to his own land . . .
> For the ships of Chittim shall come against him: there-
> fore he shall be grieved, and return, and have indignation
> against the holy covenant: so shall he do . . .
> And arms shall stand on his part, and they shall pollute
> the sanctuary of strength, and shall take away the daily sac-

rifice, and they shall place the abomination that maketh desolate (Dan. 11:28, 30, 31).

Christ speaks of this when referring to the abomination of desolation. So you see, his peace will be only for a little season and will soon be followed by war. The white horse is soon followed by the red horse spoken of in Revelation 6:

And there went out another horse that was red: and power was given him that sat thereon to take peace from the earth, and that they should kill one another: and there was given unto him a great sword (Rev. 6:4).

The peace that the Antichrist will promise will be only temporary and will be followed quickly by war, famine and death (the red, black and pale horses of Rev. 6).

THE ANTICHRIST POLITICALLY

Politically, this Man of Sin will be hailed as the master statesman of all ages. He will be the hero of the day. The league spoken of in Daniel 11 will be consummated under his leadership. The world has been looking for such a master statesman for centuries — one that would be able to weld a government together, which would be invulnerable and undefeatable. In the restored ten-toed Roman Empire (which is even now in the process of formation) in league with the Jew who holds the money, there will be a league of nations that shall be invincible until the King Himself comes and destroys them with the "brightness of his coming." The political head of the restored Roman Empire will be a figurehead. He will be called the political head, but the Antichrist will be the power behind the throne. He will work through and use as a tool the political head, while carrying out his own ends and purposes through him.

And I beheld another beast coming out of the earth; and he had two horns like a lamb, [note the imitation] and he spake as a dragon.

And he exerciseth all the power of the first beast before him, and causeth the earth and them which dwell therein to worship the first beast, whose deadly wound was healed (Rev. 13:11, 12).

THE ANTICHRIST'S RELIGION

Religiously, he will be the consummation of all lawlessness and the denial of all authority but his own. He is called the Lawless One and in the hey-day of His power he will attempt to dethrone God from His seat of power. This is ever the spirit of the Antichrist. It was the sin that caused him to be cast out of the heavens. Because the "anointed cherub" (Ezek. 28:14) exalted himself against God, he was cast from his position of power. This was again the "bait" with which he beguiled our first parents, for he promised them that they would be as God. In the last demonstration of his power he will assume the same form. As Christ declared that He was God, so, too, we see Satan again imitating the Lamb by making the same statements that He made.

> . . . the son of perdition; who opposeth himself above all that is called God, or that is worshipped; so that he as god sitteth in the temple of God, shewing himself that he is god (II Thess. 2:3, 4).
>
> And the king shall do according to his will; and he shall exalt himself, and magnify himself above every god, and shall speak marvellous things against the God of gods, and shall prosper till the indignation be accomplished: for that is determined shall be done (Dan. 11:36).

Do you doubt that the world will be ready to receive him? Atheism is one of the greatest menaces in the world today. The American Association for the Advancement of Atheism (the four A's) boldly maintains that it has millions of members in the United States and that there is no college in the land that does not have one or more of them. Thousands upon thousands of students in the high schools, colleges and universities of the land are enrolled as members. The open purpose of this Association is to do away with all religion and every teaching that sets forth the existence of God. It is the deification of man, and when that man the Antichrist comes, even if it were tomorrow, he will find the world ripe to receive him, for when he shall be revealed, he that hindereth shall be taken away and he will have free rein. If all the born-again men and women are taken out of this world there will be no opposition left.

Think of Russia today with its anti-Christian spirit of Bolshevism and Sovietism, and you have an example of how the world is being prepared for the master atheist of the last day. Let me describe an incident in point. It is almost too horrible to print.

In one of the leading papers of Moscow there appeared recently a cartoon, brightly painted in flaming colors. The central figure was Christ. Around Him were gathered a number of simple-looking individuals who were gnawing at His head and arms and legs. The bones were already denuded of flesh in places, while a priest stood beside Him, filling a cup of blood from His wounded side and drinking from a bowl of blood which he held in the other hand. The body was ripped open in the front and His bowels were gushed upon the ground; a man and a woman were drawing nourishment from the severed bowels. Underneath the cartoon were these words: "Take, Eat, This Is My Body." As we read it, we cried, "How long, O Lord, how long?" How long? That is the Antichrist; he is preparing the way for the revelation of that Man of Sin as soon as we who are His are taken out of the way.

THE ATTITUDE OF THE JEWS AND THE CHURCH

To the Jews he will proclaim himself as the promised Messiah. So clever will be this imitation, that the Jews will flock to his banner and, restored to their own land, under his feigned protection will make a covenant with him, only to have it broken off in the middle of the week.

> And he shall confirm the covenant with many for one week: and in the midst of the week he shall cause the sacrifice and the oblation to cease, and for the overspreading of abominations he shall make it desolate, even until the consummation, and that determined shall be poured upon the desolate (Dan. 9:27).

Of this Christ Himself also spoke when He said, "I am come in my Father's name, and ye receive me not: if another shall come in his own name, him ye will receive" (John 5:43). The Jew today is also ready for the Superman even though he proclaims himself to be God. A Jew said to me, "The Jews could accept a man that claimed to be God, but the Jews will never be ready to accept one who claims to be the son of God. That would mean more than one God and they will never accept that. There is only one God to the Jews and whether he be a man or God in human form, such a one might get a hearing." That is precisely what the Antichrist will do. He will deny all other gods and declare himself to be the one and only God.

Still more ready for the coming of the Antichrist is the Church in its organized form today. Men are weary of the splitting that has characterized the organized Church in all ages, both the Catholic and the Protestant. Movements are on foot in almost every group to form a union. The governing bodies of most of the denominations are considering even now overtures from other groups offering a common basis of union. Much has already been realized. The Federal Council of Churches in America is one of the first members of this product of hell. Hence those who still have a little love for the good old Gospel of the blood are slowly being squeezed and compelled to withdraw from the church systems and denominations. Within a few years, if the Lord tarries, it will be impossible to remain together. A great many of the "fence straddlers" of this day will have to get off on one side or another. Just recently the Pope issued a statement that there was but one thing for the Protestant churches to do and that was to get back in the mother church where they belonged! You may laugh at this, but the time is not far hence when this will occur. The Church of England is already Catholic, with the exception of its name. The liturgical churches are adopting confessionals and forms of absolution, while the rest are slipping into a boneless type of Modernism.

The present agitation among the churches looking toward union may be scoffed at, but it is coming. No one can stop it. It has been prophesied and it will come. Once more the scarlet woman of Revelation shall realize her dream of holding the world under her sway. That is her Catholic dream and it will be realized. We have reached the Laodicean period in this dispensation and the Master says, "Behold, I stand at the door, and knock." In the previous ages the Son of Man stood and walked among the candlesticks, but in the Laodicean period He is outside the door and calls for individual separation unto Himself. The falling away of II Thessalonians 2 is here. Soon the "Philadelphians" will be caught away, for He has promised them, "Because thou hast kept the word of my patience, I also will keep thee from the hour of temptation, which shall come upon all the world, to try them that dwell upon the earth. Behold, I come quickly, hold that fast which thou hast, that no man take thy crown" (Rev. 3:10, 11). Hallelujah!

V. THE DESTINY OF THE ANTICHRIST

The prophecy given in the third chapter of Genesis, namely, that the seed of the woman shall bruise the head of the serpent finds its complete fulfillment in the coming of the Lord. Satan shall be finally and forever cast into the lake of fire after the Millennium (Rev. 20:10). But the personal Antichrist, the tool of the devil, will meet his fate a thousand years earlier.

> And then shall that Wicked be revealed, whom the Lord will consume with the spirit of his mouth, and shall destroy with the brightness of his coming. Even him, whose coming is after the working of Satan with all power and signs and lying wonders (II Thess. 2:8-9).

> And the beast was taken, and with him the false prophet that wrought miracles before him, with which he deceived them that had received the mark of the beast, and them that worshipped his image. These both were cast alive into a lake of fire burning with brimstone (Rev. 19:20).

At the same time that the Antichrist is cast into hell, the devil will be cast into the bottomless pit for a thousand years, during which period Christ will reign here with His saints, while Israel receives all of the Lord's covenant blessings.

At the close of this dispensation of grace, the Church will be caught up, and the spirit that now hindereth will be taken out of the way. Then Satan will reveal the Antichrist, who is himself the incarnation of the devil. Then will follow the period of great tribulation, which will be shortened for the sake of the saved during this period. Then the Lord will come with His saints and the miserable career of the seed of the serpent will come to an abrupt end. His reign of terror will end at the Battle of Armageddon, when the king of the south and the king of the north and the king of the east and the king of the west will meet on their battleground in Palestine. This battle will make the last World War look like child's play. See Zech. 12:1-9; Isa. 10:28-32; Isa. 63:1-6; Jer. 25:32-38; Rev. 19:17-18; Rev. 16:14.

Reader, do you realize how near this event may be? Are you of that company that shall be spared the tribulation of those days? If you have not made your peace with God, will you do it *now*? There is still time if you are reading this, but no one can give you the assurance that you will have another opportunity tomorrow. The Spirit of God is even now gathering out a people for His Name, and when the last one of the number that he has determined has been brought in, then shall that long-looked-for day break. Those that are washed in the blood shall be caught up to be with Christ, and those that have rejected Him shall pass the darkest period in the history of this world. Remember that then "God shall send them strong delusion, that they should believe a lie: that they all might be damned who believed not the truth, but had pleasure in unrighteousness."

Friend, flee from the wrath to come before it is too late. The Saviour still waits. He offers you His salvation full and free. He paid the price. God was in Christ reconciling the world unto Himself. Now we do beseech you, "be ye reconciled to God." Come now, ere it be too late.

CHAPTER SIX

Peace in a World of War

I

Therefore being justified by faith, we have peace with God through our Lord Jesus Christ. (Romans 5:1).

Peace! What a strange ironic ring that word has in these days in which we live! The world is plunged in a bitter war of hate and greed. Peace, the dream of man in all ages, like a will-o'-the-wisp, beckons now here and now there, only to vanish in the clouds of powder smoke. Able men, wise men, great men are confessing that they are at a loss to know what the outcome will be of the present strife. There is only one answer given in all the world, however, and that answer is given by God in His precious and infallible Word.

It is not our purpose to discuss the problems of diplomacy among the nations, nor to enter into the national and international methods employed to secure a man-made peace. That is the business of those who are ordained of God to govern and rule during the absence of the final Governor and Ruler of the world, the Lord Jesus Christ. My business as a minister of the Gospel is only to preach the "thus saith the Lord" and to expound the Word of God in regard to the things which have to do with everlasting peace.

In these messages we shall discuss peace as prophesied and developed in the Word of God. We shall first present Him who is our peace and the Prince of Peace. Then we shall see that this Prince of Peace can give peace to everyone who trusts in His blood. We shall see that there can be peace only where He is, and where He is not there can be no peace; and finally we shall look to the grand, consummated, glorious peace on earth when He shall come to rule and reign in righteousness.

THE PEACE OFFERING

The Lord Jesus Christ is the Prince of Peace. In Scripture He is offered as the only hope for peace, whether in the life of the individual or in the life of nations and the world. Where He is rejected there can be no peace. In the first five chapters of the book of Leviticus we have five offerings in their order as follows:

1. The Whole Burnt Offering—Lev. 1.
2. The Meal Offering—Lev. 2.
3. The Peace Offering—Lev. 3.
4. The Sin Offering—Lev. 4.
5. The Trespass Offering—Lev. 5.

In these five offerings we have in type the complete and finished work of the Lord Jesus Christ for sinners. The number "five" is the number of the grace of God. In these five ceremonial offerings of Israel we have the typical revelation of God's complete and finished provision for the sin of mankind, and the only key to peace in the heart, as well as peace on earth. These five offerings are divided into three parts. The first two offerings represent God's provision in the Person of Christ for the sin question and have to do with the life and death of Jesus Christ to save sinners. The result of this is "peace with God." The last two offerings (the sin and the trespass offerings) have nothing to do with the sinner but, rather, with the saint. They are God's provision for the "sins of the saints"; those who were sinners but have been saved by the provision for salvation in the burnt and meal offerings. In other words, the first two offerings are for the sin of the sinner, whereas the last two are God's provision for the sins of the saints (saved sinners). These two groups are united by the peace offering. The appropriation of the first two results in "peace with God" and brings justification for the sinner. The appropriation of the last two results in the "peace of God" and produces sanctification. Bearing this division in mind, let us

examine the five offerings briefly and see what Christ is
to all them that believe.

THE WHOLE BURNT OFFERING

Not only do we believe that the content of Scripture is
divinely and inerrantly inspired, but we believe that the
order in which the record is given and the events are
recorded is inspired and has a deep and important teaching. Consider, for instance, the order of the five books of
Moses. We believe the order of Genesis, Exodus, Leviticus, Numbers and Deuteronomy, is a preview or revelation of the remainder of Scripture. Genesis records the
fall of man. Exodus is the book of the redemption of
man. Leviticus is the book of the worship of man. Numbers is the book of Israel's walking in the wilderness, and
Deuteronomy is the book of the second law, or works.
Thus we have God's complete plan of redemption. First,
we have man in sin; second, God's plan of redemption;
third, redeemed man's first duty, namely, worship; fourth,
our walk in the wilderness of this world. Until we have
learned to worship, our walk will never be what it ought
to be; and fifth is the book of work, and in the same way
our work will amount to nothing until our walk is what
it should be. The greatest obstacle we meet in trying to
win men and women to Christ is the objection of the sinner, namely, there are many professing Christians who
profess to be working for God but their walk is inconsis-
tent with their testimony. Do not try to walk until you
have learned to worship, and do not try to work until
your walk is clean. That is God's order. Martha's service
was rebuked by Jesus, not because He did not want her to
serve, but because service without worship is barren. God
is more interested in our worship than in our service. He
knows that true worship will result in service, but service
without worship is vain and void. How many Christians
there are who run around trying to serve, flying about
"like chickens with their heads cut off," only to become

more of a reproach than a testimony. In their zeal they are veritable "bulls in a china shop," because they do not realize that we can do more by prayer and worship in one hour than in a year of effort in the energy of the flesh.

This divine order is further illustrated in the five offerings. The burnt offering comes first. In it an animal was slain by the priest and placed upon the altar in the court of the Tabernacle. The characteristic of this offering was that it was called the whole burnt offering. While part of the other offerings was given to the priest and the offerer (they that served at the altar were "partakers of the altar"), not so with this first one. Not a shred of it was given to the priest or anyone else. It was to be burnt whole upon the altar. Every part of it was to be consumed. It represents the Cross of Calvary, the place where our redemption roots and grounds itself. The Cross is the foundation of all our redemption. That is why the Altar of Burnt Offering stood at the very entrance to the Tabernacle of the congregation. As the Israelite entered the door he met first the Altar of Burnt Offering. Until he stopped there, he could never go beyond. There was no approach to the laver or the table of shewbread or the golden candlestick, much less the Holy of Holies, until the priest had first stopped at the altar. Here the whole animal was slain and consumed. Here the blood was shed which formed the basis of everything which followed. Here upon the death of the innocent substitute rested every blessing of salvation. No wonder, then, that Satan should try to eliminate the Altar of Burnt Offering, the Cross! No wonder that infidelity levels all its attacks upon the blood and the need of an innocent substitute for the sin of man! Once the blood and the Cross are removed, everything else becomes powerless and vain. The Cross stands first in the plan of salvation.

> I must needs go home by the way of the Cross,
> There's no other way but this;

> I shall ne'er get sight of the gates of light
> If the way of the Cross I miss.

The altar blocked the way into the Tabernacle and to go through the door meant to go by the Cross. How significant the words of the Lord Jesus when He said, "I am the door." That door opened to the Cross. He said, "He that entereth not by the door . . . is a thief and a robber." To enter the Tabernacle any other way but by the door is to eliminate the altar and the Cross. No! There is no salvation apart from the Cross and the blood.

This first offering was the whole burnt offering. Man added nothing to it, and man had no part in it whatsoever. What a picture of the Saviour's work! He must bear the sin of the world alone. No one could help Him. Even in the last dread hour God hid His face as the Lord Jesus cried, "My God, my God, why hast thou forsaken me?" In the work of salvation man has no part except to receive what He (Christ) alone provided. See Him hanging there, forsaken by God and man, bearing the sin of a lost world in His own body on the tree, experiencing alone the infinite wrath of God upon sin. Well did Isaiah the prophet see this when he said, "I have trodden the winepress alone; and of the people there was none with me" (Isa. 63:3), and Peter, when he said, "Who his own self bare our sins in his own body on the tree" (I Pet. 2:24).

> Alone my Saviour bled and died
>   On Calvary's rough and cruel tree,
> That I, forever justified,
>   At peace with God might ever be.
>
> No toil of mine could ought avail,
>   No help of mine would He receive,
> Complete the offering He gave,
>   And all I do is just believe.

Christ is the whole burnt offering, dying on the Altar of the Whole Burnt Offering, to provide a ransom for sinners.

THE MEAL OFFERING

The death of Christ alone, however, was not enough to bring about peace with God. Thus, before we have the peace offering, spoken of in the third chapter of Leviticus, we must stop first at the meat offering (meal offering) in chapter 2. The burnt offering did all in making payment for sin, but it provided no righteousness to make us presentable before God. Pardoned sinners can never stand before God. They must appear before Him not as forgiven sinners but as justified saints. There must not even be a remembrance of sin. God is so holy that even the memory of sin is enough to bar a man from His presence. For this reason we must have the meal offering before full peace is established. As the burnt offering represents Christ's death, the meal offering represents His perfect life while here on earth. In this offering no blood is shed. It is bloodless. It was made of fine meal, without leaven or honey, baked with oil and frankincense.

OIL AND FRANKINCENSE

Oil, as you know, is the symbol of the Holy Spirit, and frankincense is the symbol of that which is pleasing to God. The Lord Jesus Christ during His ministry on earth came in the power of the Holy Spirit. At the beginning of His ministry He came to John to be baptized. He who had been conceived by the Holy Ghost, now was to be filled with the Holy Ghost, and as He came up out of the waters of baptism, God poured on Him the Holy Ghost in the form of a dove and accepted the pleasing fragrance of His obedient act by calling from heaven, "This is my beloved Son, in whom I am well pleased" (Matt. 3:17). The Lord was then ready as a man to begin His work.

NO HONEY OR LEAVEN

At His baptism Christ declared His willingness to do God's will in providing a salvation for sinners. By His temptation in the wilderness He proved His ability to defeat Satan, and by His life He demonstrated that He was able to provide a perfect human righteousness which should be imputed to poor lost sinners on the basis of His atoning work on Calvary. Remembering that the meal offering represents the life of Christ, we see the significance of the prohibition of honey and leaven. Honey is symbolic of the sweets of life. The good things of the earth which we love and which God wants us to enjoy were never experienced by our great meal offering. He came "despised and rejected of men; a man of sorrows, and acquainted with grief." He never had a home of His own. Wearing a borrowed garment, He depended on the generosity of His friends for His sustenance. To pay His taxes He had to send Peter fishing. He could say, "The foxes have holes, and the birds of the air have nests; but the Son of man hath not where to lay his head." He was poor and needy — the extras of life and friends were never His portion. He was the offering without the sweeter things, the honey of life.

Then, too, there was no leaven in this offering. Leaven invariably stands for evil in the Scriptures. Never once is the word "leaven" used to imply good. It is a symbol of evil in doctrine or evil in practice. Jesus speaks of the leaven of the Pharisees and the Sadducees (doctrinal leaven). Paul speaks of the leaven of wickedness and malice (moral leaven). Neither of these were in the meal offering. Jesus Christ was the only perfect Man since the fall of Adam. The spies sent by the Pharisees to trap Him came back without evidence. No accusations could be found against Him, and they had to bribe false witnesses to indict Him. Even then, Pilate, speaking for humanity, had to say, "I find no fault in him." He was the perfect meal offering.

> O blessed offering, God's only Son,
> Who there for us salvation won,
> No sin or guilt to call His own,
> For others' guilt He must atone.

> No leaven in Him e'er was found
> But previous meal and finely ground,
> No honeyed pleasures were His lot,
> But our dark sin He came to blot.

The death of Christ made payment for sin. It saves us from hell, but still cannot fit us for heaven. When Christ died He made payment for sin and those who believe will never be lost, but if no more had been done, man, though saved from hell through faith, could not enter heaven. He would be a forgiven sinner and no more. Therefore, to fit him for heaven as well, Jesus provided righteousness with which He clothes the forgiven sinner and imputes to Him His Own perfect righteousness. We are saved from sin by His death and saved for heaven by His life. Why did Jesus have to live thirty-three years before He went to the Cross? Why did He not come to the world as Adam did, a full-grown man, and immediately go to Calvary? It would have spared Him the reproach and reviling of thirty-three years. Friend, God is so holy that merely paying for sin was not enough. There must be a righteousness provided, a human righteousness as well as a divine righteousness. This Christ did when He lived to mature manhood in perfect righteousness and kept the law of God entirely. When we come to Him by faith, He imputes to us His death by which our sins are put away, and then He also imputes to us His righteousness; He "wraps us up," as it were, in His own righteousness, so that when God looks upon us He sees us in Christ, not as pardoned sinners, but as men and women in Christ, as perfect as though we had never committed a single sin but had always lived as perfectly as the One in whose garment we are arrayed.

THE PEACE OFFERING

Now follows the peace offering, and not until now. When we accept Christ by faith He becomes our substitute in death and our righteousness in life. "Therefore being justified by faith, we have peace with God through

our Lord Jesus Christ." God accepts us in Him as perfect
and holy; as though we had never sinned. Sinner, will
you accept this peace? There is nothing to do but receive Him by faith.

II
THE SIN AND THE TRESPASS OFFERING

We have discussed the whole burnt offering as repre-
senting the death of Christ upon the Cross for the sin of
man. By this offering the penalty of sin was borne by the
Lord Jesus Christ and now all who believe on Him are
free from the penalty of sin, eternal death and woe. More
was needed, however, than merely salvation from hell.
Provision must also be made for our acceptance into God's
presence. This, we saw, was provided by the same person
to which the five offerings in Leviticus point. The second of these five offerings in Leviticus, the meal offering,
is a type of the perfect humanity of the Lord Jesus Christ.
This perfect righteousness is imputed to all who by faith
have believed on Him and have been delivered from the
judgment of God. The result of this is the peace offering
whereby the sinner is at peace with God through our
Lord and Saviour Jesus Christ.

Before considering the last two offerings in Leviticus
1-5, permit me to list them again in their exact order, for
the order in which they occur is as important as the offerings themselves. In the first five chapters of Leviticus
we have five offerings, one for each chapter. They are in
their order as follows:

1. The Whole Burnt Offering—chap. 1.
2. The Meal or Meat Offering—chap. 2.
3. The Peace Offering—chap. 3.
4. The Sin Offering—chap. 4.
5. The Trespass Offering—chap. 5.

The first two have to do with God's provision for the
sinner and result in justification. The last two have to do
with the sins of the saints after they are saved, and result

in sanctification. The result of the first group is peace with God, and the result of the second group is the peace of God which passeth understanding.

THE NEED FOR SIN OFFERINGS

When the Lord Jesus Christ came to die on the Cross for our sin, He not only knew what great sinners we were, but He also knew what terrible failures we would be after we were saved. He knew that we would not be able to keep ourselves, in our own strength, and if He made no provisions for our constant cleansing after we had accepted Him we would not remain saved a single day or hour. He knew the frailty of human nature, and since He gives eternal life He also makes provision for eternal life. In the same Christ who saves us we have One also who keeps us. By studying carefully the peace offering in Leviticus 3 you will notice that two parts of the peace offering — the shoulder and the breast — were to be given to the priest. The shoulder is a symbol of power and strength, and the breast is the symbol of nourishment and sustenance. Both these are provided in Him who became our peace offering on the basis of the blood of the burnt offering and the righteousness of the meal offering. While we have peace with God because of His work for us, the peace of God is ours only as we exercise the power of a cleansed life and feed daily upon Him who is both our food and drink; the Lamb who was slain for our sins and then became the Passover Lamb to feed us during our journey through the wilderness.

TWO KINDS OF CHRISTIANS

The Bible classifies Christians as *carnal* or *spiritual*. The carnal Christian is one who has accepted Christ, appropriated Him as substitute and righteousness and is thereby at peace with God. However, the carnal Christian has never truly appropriated Him as the sin and tresspass offering, thereby receiving the peace of God. There are victorious Christians and there are defeated

Christians. Jesus said, "I am come that they might have life." That is one thing. Then He adds, "That they might have it more abundantly." That is another thing. We may be in the light and be saved, but we are admonished also to "walk in the light, as he is in the light." We come to Christ for salvation but we come after Him for service. Jesus said in John 4, to the woman at the well:

> Whosoever drinketh of this water shall thirst again: but whosoever drinketh of the water that I shall give him shall never thirst; but the water that I shall give him shall be in him a well of water springing up into everlasting life (John 4:13, 14).

It is one thing to have the water of life in you, but that is not all. In John 7 Jesus says:

> He that believeth on me, as the scripture hath said, out of his belly shall flow rivers of living water.

That is quite another thing. In the first instance, the man has eternal life in Him, but that eternal life does not profit anyone else. This life must flow out of Him and refresh the lives of others. The first is salvation, the second, the fruit of salvation. There is a baptism in the Spirit for salvation and a filling with the Spirit for service.

When we accept Christ as our burnt and meal offering, we receive the first, and have peace with God, but it is not until we appropriate Him as our sin and trespass offering that we experience the second. The last two offerings in Leviticus, then, are God's provision for the saints. We need to stop only once at the burnt offering — only once to be saved — but we fail to go to Him as our offering to be cleansed and forgiven, thus to be fitted for renewed service. It is the failure of Christians to confess their sins and receive the cleansing that makes for the deadness and fruitlessness of the average believer.

THREE CLASSES OF SINS

One must carefully distinguish between sin and sins. The sin refers to the sinner. Sins are those acts committed by the believer after his salvation. John says in I

John 1: "If we [believers] confess our sins, he is faithful
and just to forgive us our sins, and to cleanse us from all
unrighteousness." If you turn to the fourth and fifth
chapters of Leviticus you will notice that three kinds of
sins are mentioned for which provision is made in these
offerings. Notice first Leviticus 4:

> Speak unto the children of Israel, saying, If a soul shall
> sin through ignorance against any of the commandments of
> the Lord concerning things which ought not to be done,
> and shall do against any of them . . . let him bring for his
> sin, which he hath sinned, a young bullock without blemish
> unto the Lord for a sin offering (Lev. 4:2, 3).

Now notice the second of the sins (Lev. 5:1):

> And if a soul sin, and hear the voice of swearing, and is a
> witness, whether he hath seen or known of it; if he do not
> utter it, then he shall bear his iniquity.

Then follows the third of the sins (Lev. 5:2):

> Or if a soul touch any unclean thing, whether it be a
> carcase of an unclean beast, or a carcase of unclean cattle,
> or the carcase of unclean creeping things, and if it be hidden
> from him; he also shall be unclean, and guilty.

For these three classes of sins a sacrifice was provided
and the guilty Israelite was to bring the sacrifice, lay his
hand in confession upon its head, and deliver it to the
priest, whereupon his sins were forgiven him. Notice
that these three classes of sins were:

1. Sins of Ignorance.
2. Sins of Omission.
3. Sins of Defilement.

SINS OF IGNORANCE

God is a holy God. Failure to recognize His holiness
leads ever to a false sense of our own holiness. The more
a man boasts of his own holiness, the less he knows of
God's holiness. The more a man realizes the holiness of
God, the more he will see his own vileness, and the more
reluctant he will be to boast of his own goodness. God is
so holy that He cannot permit even sins of ignorance to go
unheeded but provided a sacrifice for them as well. How
happy we, as believers, ought to be about this. Sins of
ignorance are sins of which we have no knowledge or

conscience. How many things you and I have done in the past, possibly in the early days of Christian experience, only to find later on as we read our Bibles and learned God's will that these things and practices were wrong! Because we had not been better instructed and because we did not have the full teaching and light on .matters of life, we practiced sins of which we were unaware. Then when the Word of God revealed the truth of these sins to our minds and hearts, what a joy it was to find that God knew beforehand what stumbling failures we would be and He had made provision with the blood of the sin offering for our cleansing the moment we came. Since none of us have perfect knowledge as yet, how important that each day the Christian should confess the sins of ignorance. This thought is expressed in that beautiful song called "Evening Prayer":

> Forgive the sins I have confessed to Thee;
> Forgive, dear Lord, the secret sins I cannot see.

The writer of those lines evidently realized the provision that had been made in the sin offering, for the sins we did not know we had committed.

SINS OF OMISSION

The second class of sins we find mentioned in the fifth chapter. They are the sins of "omission." They are the things we should have done but have not done: our failure to stand up for Christ when His Name was reviled; our failure to seek to win others to Christ; our failure to be as fervent as we ought in prayer; the opportunities we have wasted, opportunities that never will return. How we permitted the weariness of our flesh and the fear of man to keep us from being our best! All that is sin. I wonder whether those who boast of their holiness realize that sin is not only doing wrong things but also failure to do all the right things. For these sins, too, the Lord made provision in Christ, our trespass offering, and all we need to do to be cleansed is to present Him again as our offering and then "if we confess our sins, he is faithful and just to forgive us our sins, and to cleanse us from all unrighteousness." Our dear Lord recognized how frail we would be and took the weakness of His children into consideration when He provided the sacrifice on the Cross for us.

SINS OF DEFILEMENT

In the third group of sins of the believers found in Leviticus 5 are the sins of defilement. The Israelite might not even know that he had touched an unclean thing, but he was guilty just the same. God is holy — so holy that not one tiny spot goes unnoticed. We are living in a corrupt world. In our social, business and even religious life we are constantly brushing shoulders with unclean things. Is there a businessman who would dare to say that he can do business as a Christian in this world and not be defiled? You Christians have to deal with ungodly salesmen and customers. Some of you work for ungodly employers, in places where the very atmosphere reeks with smut and profanity. There is nothing you can do about it without casting your pearls before the swine. It defiles you, nevertheless, and you need cleansing. Our blessed Lord knew how hard it was going to be for you to live in this wicked world and try to make a livelihood under these conditions. He knew how difficult and impossible it would be to remain undefiled, and while He does not justify defilement, He does make provision for it. To become daily defiled is sin even though unavoidable, but failure to avail yourself of the cleansing provided is inexcusable, and will result in the sure judgment of God. Since He has been gracious enough to provide a cleansing, surely you cannot expect to go unpunished if you despise His provision.

THE CLEANSING

For each of these sins a sacrifice was provided. For one it was a bullock, for another a goat, etc. All of these sacrifices pointed to Him, our blessed High Priest, and all spoke of His blood. The Israelite was to lay his hand on the head of the sacrifice, thereby confessing his sin, and then the priest did the rest. O Christian, have you learned the victory that Christ offers when you yield everything over to Him? Paul says in Philippians:

> Be careful for nothing; but in every thing by prayer and supplication with thanksgiving let your requests be made known unto God.
> And the peace of God, which passeth all understanding, shall keep your hearts and minds through Christ Jesus (Phil. 4:6, 7).

Are you defeated and discouraged? Then confess to Him and accept His promise that "if we confess our sins, he is faithful and just to forgive us our sins, and to cleanse us from all unrighteousness." When you have confessed, then trust Him. Do not be anxious any more, but having done your part, leave the rest to Him. Do not confess your sin more than once to Him. Many people confess the same sin over and over again, thereby insulting God. If you have confessed it once, then believe that He keeps His word. If we confess, He forgives. To confess the same sin again is to tell God you do not believe He forgave you the first time. Bring your sin offering in confession and then leave the rest with the Priest. Go away with thanksgiving instead of doubt. "Be careful for nothing; but in every thing by prayer and supplication with thanksgiving let your requests be made known"; then "the peace of God which passeth all understanding" will keep your heart and mind through Christ Jesus.

Thousands of Christians are defeated, sad and powerless because they let their sins bother them instead of confessing them. Look away from your failures and look to Christ, He who died to save your life and to cleanse you. Do not grieve Him longer by doubting His word. "Take your burdens to the Lord and leave them there."

Confess that sin of unbelief and doubt now. Tell Him you have grieved Him by letting the sins you have confessed continue to bother you.

Here is an illustration. Two Israelites have brought an offering for a trespass, laid their hands upon the sacrifice and delivered it to the priest. One goes away happy, the other is more gloomy than before. Both are equally safe. Both are equally forgiven, but one is happy and the other is sad. Do you know the difference? One has trusted his all to the priest. Having done all that he could do, namely, confessed his sin and brought his offering, he goes away happy. The other has done the same thing, and his offering is accepted, too, but he is sad. Do you know why? He is afraid the priest may make a slip or an error in presenting the blood and his confession will not avail. That priest in the tabernacle in the wilderness might make a mistake, but listen, listen, your Priest in heaven will never make a mistake. Trust Him. Trust Him. Kneel where you are and confess your greatest sin, which perhaps is the sin of not trusting Him.

Christ is our offering for sin. When you were saved you believed His word. That was all. Christ is also our offering for *sins*, which we as believers commit, and He knew we would commit them. Trust Him for your cleansing just as you did for your salvation.

If we confess our sins, he is faithful and just to forgive us our sins, and to cleanse us from all unrighteousness.

III

And suddenly there was with the angel a multitude of the heavenly host praising God, and saying, Glory to God in the highest, and on earth peace, good will toward men (Luke 2:13, 14).

Thus did the angels herald the birth of the Lord Jesus Christ, the Prince of Peace, some nineteen hundred years ago. Yet after almost two millenniums the words of the angels have not been fulfilled, for from that day until this there has been no peace, but rather war, hatred, bloodshed, hell and destruction. With very brief and very few intermissions this old world has been soaked in the blood of humanity, and its tranquillity has been disturbed by the incessant battle cry of nations in commotion. Were the angels, then, mistaken when they chanted "Peace on earth and good will toward men"? On the surface it would appear that they were, for the coming of the Prince of Peace has not yet brought "peace" among the nations and good will among men on earth.

Some thirty years after the angels announced this "peace on earth" the one of whom they spoke said something that seemed to indicate that the angels were mistaken. Listen to the words of the Lord Jesus Christ in Matthew 10:34-36:

> Think not that I am come to send peace on earth: I came not to send peace, but a sword. For I am come to set a man at variance against his father, and the daughter against her mother, and the daughter-in-law against her mother-in-law. And a man's foes shall be they of his own household.

As the Lord Jesus approached the end of His earthly ministry, He gathered His followers about Him again and again to warn them that, after His ministry was ended here, there would not follow an age of peace and increasing good will among men, but on the very contrary there would follow an age that would be characterized by hatred, violence, bloodshed and war, ending finally in the greatest holocaust of all ages — the near destruction of civilization. This is the unbroken testimony of Scripture, but nowhere is it more explicitly and simply stated than in the very words of our Lord just before He went to the Cross. He had said in the beginning of His ministry, "Think not that I am come to send peace . . . I came not to send peace, but a sword," and as His ministry drew to a close He said:

> Take heed that no man deceive you. For many shall come in my name, saying, I am Christ: and shall deceive many. And ye shall hear of wars and rumours of wars: see that ye be not troubled: for all these things must come to pass

but the end is not yet. For nation shall rise against nation, and kingdom against kingdom: and there shall be famines, and pestilences, and earthquakes, in divers places.

All these are the beginning of sorrows.

Then shall they deliver you up to be afflicted, and shall kill you: and ye shall be hated of all nations for my name's sake.

And then shall many be offended, and shall betray one another, and shall hate one another. And many false prophets shall rise, and shall deceive many.

And because iniquity shall abound, the love of many shall wax cold (Matt. 24:4-12).

This is the picture which the Lord Jesus Himself gives of this age, which was ushered in by His death on the Cross. According to our Lord's words, wickedness and war shall increase until they reach their climax at the end of the age. It is not a picture of peace and good will among men in any sense of the word. In addition to the above passages we might turn to a host of others, both in the Old Testament and the New Testament, to show that the unbroken testimony of the Word is, that during this dispensation things will become worse and worse, finally to end in the Battle of Armageddon, at which time man will annihilate himself were it not for the sudden intervention of God in the return of the Lord Jesus Christ. Then and then only will there be peace on earth and good will toward men.

WERE THE ANGELS WRONG?

So we ask the question again: Were the angels mistaken when they hailed the birth of Jesus with "Peace on earth and good will to men"? The answer lies in the correct interpretation of prophecy and the recognition of God's dispensational dealings. The angels did announce "peace on earth" at the coming of the Prince of Peace. Man, however, did not accept the Prince of Peace but, instead, misunderstood His mission and put Him to death on the Cross. As a result, the Prince of Peace was rejected and the peace foretold by the prophets and announced by the angels was postponed until the time when the world would acknowledge Him. The peace the angels offered was conditional upon man's accepting the Prince of Peace. But John says:

> He was in the world, and the world was made by him, and the world knew him not. He came unto his own, and his own received him not (John 1:10, 11).

All this was foreknown of God, and His written Word takes into consideration the rejection by the people of the Prince of Peace. When John the Baptist came his message was: "Repent . . . for the kingdom of heaven is at hand." The King was in their very midst, offering Israel the kingdom, but they received Him not. They rejected Him. So the kingdom offered them by John and the disciples was postponed, and Christ, instead of setting up the kingdom, went to the Cross. The peace the angels announced was postponed until that time when the Prince of Peace should come again and be acknowledged by His own. Then that glad day will be ushered in of which all Christians sing:

> Jesus shall reign where'er the sun
> Does his successive journeys run;
> His kingdom spread from shore to shore,
> Till moons shall wax and wane no more.
> From north to south the princes meet
> To pay their homage at His feet;
> While western empires own their Lord,
> And savage tribes attend His word.

No, the angels were not mistaken. They announced the birth of the Prince of Peace and promised "peace on earth" if He would be accepted. There can be no peace without the Lord Jesus Christ. Where He is there is peace. Where He is not there can be no peace. It is a remarkable fact that during the thirty-three years that Jesus was on the earth, history does not record one battle among the nations. While the Prince of Peace was here there was peace. Before He came there was incessant war, and since He departed there has been war somewhere in the world. Only the presence of the Lord Jesus Christ can bring peace. Well did the angels announce "peace."

Soon after the Lord Jesus began His ministry on earth

it became apparent that the nation of Israel would not accept her King, but, rather, would reject Him. It is after He sends forth His disciples in Matthew 10 that Jesus predicts that they will not be received by the people, but that instead, the people will reject their message. It is then that He makes the announcement: "Think not that I am come to send peace."

God has a plan, based upon His perfect foreknowledge, which He designed from eternity. According to His plan the King was to come to His people and offer the kingdom. They would reject. As a result the King would reject His people and cause them to be scattered to wander among the nations until the time should come for them to acknowledge and receive Him. Then the long prophesied millennial kingdom would be set up and "peace on earth" would follow. Included in this great plan for the ages was also the Church of Jesus Christ. This is the mystery hidden in the Old Testament to be revealed only after God had rejected Israel upon their crucifixion of their King. According to this eternal plan God permitted Israel to reject her Lord and then set her aside, during which time He would gather out from among the nations a people for His Name and glory. These people would be destined to be the bride of the King during the Kingdom Age. Thus the nation to whom Christ came is "set aside" while He is calling out the Church (His bride). When the fullness of the Gentiles be come in, the Lord will return with His bride. Then Israel "shall look upon him whom they pierced"; they will receive their Messiah, and "peace on earth" will become a reality. Listen to Paul in Romans 11:25-27:

> For I would not, brethren, that ye should be ignorant of this mystery, lest ye should be wise in your own conceits, that blindness in part is happened to Israel, until the fulness of the Gentiles be come in.
> And so all Israel shall be saved: as it is written, There shall come out of Sion the Deliverer, and shall turn away ungodliness from Jacob: For this is my covenant unto them, when I shall take away their sins.

Until that time comes there must be war. The hope of the Church, the individual, the world and the nations is the Lord Jesus Christ. When He comes the second time, then shall every knee bow to Him and every tongue confess that Jesus Christ is Lord to the glory of God the Father. Then the nations "shall beat their swords into plowshares, and their spears into pruninghooks: nation shall not lift up a sword against nation, neither shall they learn war any more." God haste the day!

Here is the picture. Jesus came as the Prince of Peace and was heralded as such by the angels. If Israel had received Him the first time, then Christ would have set up the kingdom and ushered in everlasting peace. But in the great plan of God, the Church, too, must be brought in and purchased by the blood of the Prince of Peace. God knew that Jesus would be rejected at His first coming; so He made the rejection of Christ by those to whom He offered the kingdom the occasion for the indispensable death of the Lord and the shedding of His blood on which the salvation of the Church and abiding peace could be founded.

PEACE IN HEAVEN

There is peace, even though there is no evidence of it among the nations. Wherever Jesus is there is peace. Wherever He is not there is war. While He was here on earth there was peace on earth. Even the wild waves obeyed His voice when He said, "Peace be still." Now He has gone to heaven and there is peace in heaven, for where He is there is peace. Notice what the disciples said at the last public offer of Christ to the nation as recorded in Luke 19:37, 38:

> And when he was come nigh, even now at the descent of the mount of Olives, the whole multitude of the disciples began to rejoice and praise God with a loud voice for all the mighty works that they had seen;
>
> Saying, Blessed be the King that cometh in the name of the Lord: Peace in heaven, and glory in the highest.

Notice those words: "Peace in heaven." They do not say as the angels did "Peace on earth." That peace on earth was at the beginning of His work here. If the King had been received then, there would have been peace on earth. But now the King has been rejected by the leaders and He is on His way to the Cross instead of the Throne. The Holy Spirit must have put these prophetic words into the mouths of the disciples as they shouted, "Peace in heaven." Yes, peace is not to come to the earth at this time, but He is still the Prince of Peace. In a few days He was to be nailed to the Cross, but He would still be the Prince of Peace. A few days after He would be laid in a tomb, but He would still be the Prince of Peace. Then He arose and came forth as the Prince of Peace and breathed on the disciples, saying, "Peace I leave with you, my peace I give unto you." Then the Prince of Peace, rejected by the world, went to heaven and took peace with Him and left war behind. While He is the rejected of the world there is peace in heaven. That is the only place, my friend, where you will find peace. There are only two places where peace is to be found today. There is peace in heaven because Jesus is there, and there is peace in the heart of every believer because Jesus is there as well. Where He is there is peace. Apart from Him there is no peace.

He is coming again to this earth. Israel will recognize Him and own Him, and He will bring in His kingdom of peace and righteousness when this world will know no war for one thousand years. There will be no poverty or depression, but, rather, peace among men, nature, animals, birds and fish. That day is near. Presently we shall discuss that age of peace and the things which will precede it. As we look about today we see in the darkening war clouds the outlines of the age of peace. It is near and Jesus said, "When ye shall see all these things, know that it is near, even at the doors."

PEACE IN YOUR HEART

You, individually, may have peace now in the midst of this world at war. It can be had — perfect peace — by letting the Prince of Peace into your heart.

> Behold, I stand at the door and knock: if any man hear my voice, and open the door, I will come in to him and will sup with him (Rev. 3:20).
> Therefore being justified by faith, we have peace with God through our Lord Jesus Christ (Rom. 5:1).
> Thou wilt keep him in perfect peace, whose mind is stayed on thee: because he trusteth in thee (Isa. 26:3).

As the war clouds loom, the thunderous cannon boom and men's hearts are failing them, you can have peace — the peace that comes when you accept the Prince of Peace as your Saviour. Then you have peace because you know your sins are forgiven and no matter what happens, you are saved for eternity. You will have peace because you know that all that is happening is according to a plan and a purpose, and that God is still on the throne. You will know that He is making the wrath of man to praise Him and setting the stage for the coming of the Prince of Peace. If you know Him, then you have peace because you know that soon He will come back again to bring peace to this troubled world. God haste the day when "he that shall come will come, and will not tarry."

IV

> But in the last days it shall come to pass, that the mountain of the house of the Lord shall be established in the top of the mountains, and it shall be exalted above the hills; and people shall flow unto it.
> And many nations shall come, and say, Come, and let us go up to the mountain of the Lord, and to the house of the God of Jacob; and he will teach us of his ways, and we will walk in his paths: for the law shall go forth of Zion, and the word of the Lord from Jerusalem.
> And he shall judge among many people, and rebuke strong nations afar off; and they shall beat their swords into plowshares, and their spears into pruninghooks: nation shall not lift up a sword against nation, neither shall they learn war any more.
> But they shall sit every man under his vine and under his fig tree; and none shall make them afraid: for the mouth of the Lord of hosts hath spoken it (Micah. 4:1-4).

The universal cry of the human heart in these days in which we are living is for *peace* — not merely a cessation of hostilities for a time, not merely an armistice, which is but a breathing spell for the next battle, but an abiding and lasting peace, when the wealth of the nations shall not be dissipated in building armaments but be used for the happiness and enjoyment of mankind. This abiding peace is the dream of nations today. Some think it will come in one way, others are fighting to get it in another way. Yet, the warring nations still dream of peace.

GOD'S PROMISE

The Bible teaches in an unbroken chain of prophecies that such a golden age of peace is coming. The passage at the head of this message is but one of hundreds in the Word of the Lord which testifies to the fact that in the program of God there will come an age of blessedness and peace when all the world will be at rest under the dominion and sway of the Prince of Peace. This age of peace cannot come, however, until God's own time and until His program has run its course and all His prophecies have been fulfilled. Any peace contrary to the foreordained program of God is doomed to failure. Any lasting peace without the Prince of Peace is a product of man's wishful thinking and idle dreams. Nevertheless, that age is coming in due time when the kingdoms of this earth shall become the kingdoms of our Lord and of His Christ.

WAR FIRST . . . THEN PEACE

Before this age of peace and prosperity comes, however, there will be a time of war and destruction eclipsing all others in history. There is not one verse in the Bible nor one iota of proof in Scripture that this golden age will be ushered in by the Church or nations or men. For many years there have been those who taught that by the gradual dissemination of the so-called "leaven" of the Gospel, education, reformation and better understanding among the nations and peoples, this age would get better and better, until finally, by man's efforts and preaching, the world would learn its lesson. Nations would settle differences on the basis of the Golden Rule and the Sermon on the Mount, and then would follow the Millennium; after the Millennium the Lord would come to judge the world. This theory is called *Postmillennialism* because it postpones the coming of the Lord until after the Millennium. That theory, however, and that sort of wishful thinking has received a very rude shock in the last few decades. Just when man thought he had made some advance, the last World War broke out with its brutality, barbarism and its list of millions upon millions of casualties. Yet man continued to hope. There followed prohibition in this land and the exponents of the "post-millennial - pull - yourself - up - by - your - own - boot-straps" theory raised a great cry and said, "See how we have progressed. We have conquered the demon Rum and soon we shall slay the devil War." But that exuberance, too, was short-lived, for after a few years of questionable drouth, the demon Rum was let loose again. Like the evil spirit in the parable, the demon Rum, after he had wandered in dry places, came back and found the house swept, garnished but empty, went out and found seven spirits more wicked than himself and came back with a vengeance and the latter end is worse than the first. Our Lord might well have been thinking of American prohibition and repeal when He gave this parable, for like the house of the evil spirit, this land was cursed by the demon Rum. Then we cast him out but let the house empty. Instead of asking Christ to move in we only put out the demon. He wandered in dry places for some years and then came back when we repealed prohibition, and from the number of taverns, road houses, saloons, grocery stores, oil stations, drug stores and restaurants which now sell the devil's concoction, liquor, we suspect that this demon outdid the demon in Christ's parable, for instead of bringing back seven demons more wicked than himself, he has brought back seventy.

Later there followed an era in which men talked of peace. There were conferences, treaties, limitation of armaments, the League of Nations and trade pacts. The "Posts" took heart once more, and hoped that their dream of peace by "human" effort and dissemination of the Gospel would work. Then came the explosion in Asia and then in Europe shattering all the fondest hopes of the "idealistic Postmills" into a thousand fragments and driving them helter-skelter into the flimsy haven of "Amillennialism."

THE BIBLE'S ANSWER

The Bible, however, testifies invariably to an entirely different program. There is not one verse in Scripture that says that this age will end in peace; it will end, rather, in war. There is not proof in the Bible that as we approach the end of this age, morally, economically, socially, internationally, religiously, conditions will become better; but, rather, that they will all get worse. Jesus says, in describing the days just before the close of this dispensation (read Matthew 24:6, 7):

> And ye shall hear of wars and rumours of wars . . . For nation shall rise up against nation, and kingdom against kingdom: and there shall be famines, and pestilences, and earthquakes, in divers places.

What is true of nations is true also in the moral realm, for the Apostle Paul tells us what will prevail in the last days in these words (read II Timothy 3:1-5):

> This know also, that in the last days perilous times shall come. For men shall be lovers of their own selves, covetous, boasters, proud, blasphemers, disobedient to parents, unthankful, unholy, without natural affection, trucebreakers, false accusers, incontinent, fierce, despisers of those that are good, traitors, heady, highminded, lovers of pleasures more than lovers of God; having a form of godliness, but denying the power thereof.

Religiously, it will be a time of apostasy. The whole testimony of Scripture is that just before the coming of the Lord the professing Church will fall into worldliness, leave the preaching of the Gospel to turn to politics, moral reform and the preaching of a bloodless social gospel. Read what Paul says in II Timothy 4:

> For the time will come when they will not endure sound doctrine; but after their own lusts shall they heap to themselves teachers, having itching ears; And they shall turn away their ears from the truth, and shall be turned unto fables (II Tim. 4:3, 4).

Listen to Paul as he writes to his son Timothy in the First Epistle of Timothy:

> Now the Spirit speaketh expressly, that in the latter times some shall depart from the faith, giving heed to seducing spirits and doctrines of devils;
> Speaking lies in hypocrisy; having their conscience seared with a hot iron;
> Forbidding to marry, and commanding to abstain from meats, which God hath created to be received with thanksgiving of them which believe and know the truth (I Tim. 4:1-3).

We might continue to quote Scripture passages telling us that this age will end in war, apostasy, falling away, until it seems that Christianity, morality and civilization will disappear from the earth. But all this is according to God's foreknown program. God will allow man to prove that the human heart is and remains "deceitful above all things, and desperately wicked," no matter how much you educate or cultivate it. The only hope is Christ, the Prince of Peace. Men and women, when are we going to learn that everything must fail until we yield to Him?

> Even the youths shall faint and be weary, and the young men shall utterly fall:
> But they that wait upon the Lord shall renew their strength; they shall mount up with wings as eagles; they shall run, and not be weary; and they shall walk, and not faint (Isaiah 40:30, 31).

GOD'S PROGRAM

Let us turn now from man's futile program and see the program of God. The next event in God's program will be the catching away of the Church in the Rapture. This to be followed by the Battle of Armageddon and the coming of the Lord with His Church to set up the kingdom of universal peace. Of the many, many passages in Scripture, let me quote one in Joel 3:

> For, behold, in those days and in that time [referring to the end of this age described in the previous chapter Joel 2], when I shall bring again the captivity of Judah and Jerusalem, I will also gather all nations, and will bring them down into the valley of Jehoshaphat, and will plead with them there for my people and for my heritage Israel (Joel 3:1, 2).

Notice the message the Lord commands us to proclaim in these last days. It may surprise some of you that the Lord commands us to tell the nations to prepare for war. Men ask, "Should Christians support the 'defense program' "? The answer is clear if we know the program of the last days. There is nothing else to do. Of all the people in the land who should preach "defense" and proclaim the necessity of a huge defense program, the Christians should be first. Listen to this passage from Joel 3:

> Proclaim ye this among the Gentiles; Prepare war, wake up the mighty men, let all the men of war draw near; let them come up: beat your plowshares into swords, and your pruninghooks into spears: let the weak say, I am strong. Assemble yourselves, and come, all ye heathen, and gather yourselves together round about: thither cause thy mighty ones to come down, O Lord (Joel 3:9-11).

We are beholding the very fulfillment of these words before our eyes. Plowshares and pruninghooks are being turned into swords and spears. We are turning the implements of agriculture into instruments of war. Factories and industries heretofore engaged in the production of machinery for pleasure and industry have become munitions plants in the defense program. It is all Scriptural. God commanded Joel to proclaim it among the nations. When the world is fully armed, every nation is involved, the armies are completed and the whole world an arsenal, then will come the great battle for which the world is preparing. We read in Joel 3:14, 15:

> Multitudes, multitudes in the valley of decision: for the day of the Lord is near in the valley of decision. The sun and the moon shall be darkened, and the stars shall withdraw their shining.

This darkening of sun, moon and stars will probably be the result of the clouds of smoke from the holocaust, caused by the clouds of planes which will set the very world on fire. Then — when it verily seems that civilization will perish and man will annihilate himself — then will come the next event. Read the verse following in Joel:

> The Lord also shall roar out of Zion, and utter his voice from Jerusalem; and the heavens and the earth shall shake: but the Lord will be the hope of his people, and the strength of the children of Israel (Joel 3:16).

PEACE ON EARTH

This will be the end of the battle. The Lord Jesus Christ will suddenly return to the earth, punish the nations which now oppress, liberate the peoples now chafing under the cruel yoke of the oppressors, bring all Israel back to the land of Palestine, and then Jesus shall sit on the throne to rule and reign. Notice the peaceful description in these verses from Joel and Isaiah:

> And it shall come to pass in that day, that the mountains shall drop down new wine, and the hills shall flow with milk, and all the rivers of Judah shall flow with waters, and a fountain shall come forth of the house of the Lord (Joel 3:18).
> The wolf also shall dwell with the lamb, and the leopard shall lie down with the kid; and the calf and the young lion and the fatling together; and a little child shall lead them.
> And the cow and the bear shall feed; their young ones shall lie down together: and the lion shall eat straw like the ox.
> And the sucking child shall play on the hole of the asp, and the weaned child shall put his hand on the cockatrice' den.
> They shall not hurt nor destroy in all my holy mountain: for the earth shall be full of the knowledge of the Lord, as the waters cover the sea (Isa. 11:6-9).

God haste that glad day when:

> Christ shall have dominion over land and sea;
> Earth's remotest regions shall His empire be.
> He that shall come will come, and will not tarry.